RAYMOND IV
Count of Toulouse

Raymond IV
Count of Toulouse

JOHN HUGH HILL

LAURITA LYTTLETON HILL

SYRACUSE UNIVERSITY PRESS 1962

Library of Congress Catalog Card: 62-14120

MANUFACTURED IN THE UNITED STATES OF AMERICA

FOREWORD

WITH THE exception of Raymond IV, Count of Toulouse, the important leaders of the First Crusade have had their exploits recorded biographically in English. Professor A. C. Krey called attention to this lacuna some years ago, and it is our hope that this monograph supplies the lack.

To understand the Count of Toulouse, it has been necessary to understand his chroniclers, a task carried beyond this biography. With the generous support of the American Philosophical Society, we have continued to observe the methods of Raymond d'Aguilers, self-styled chronicler of Raymond IV. From Raymond d'Aguilers' work we have gone on to that of Petrus Tudebodus, and with the help of Walter E. Singer we hope to carry the study to Albert of Aachen.

This biography of Raymond IV is a result of critical examination of the sources and the realization that the main objectives of the Count of Toulouse were often concealed by the hagiographical excursions of Raymond d'Aguilers. We have attempted to show that the Count of Toulouse was true to the ideal of the First Crusade. The long misunderstanding of his role may be explained in part by the many centuries of hatred and prejudice which marked sectional differences in France, and in part by the eagerness of historians to oversimplify human motivation.

The eleventh century, like the twentieth century, was marked by crusading interests. Hidden under multifarious motives, in the eleventh century the magic lay in the recovery of the Holy Sepulcher. Today the magic lies in economic and political ideology. Those who in the twentieth century strive for economic and political ideals may reflect that they have much in common with the Count of Toulouse, who, in the eleventh century, with the inspiration of his Holy Quest, with toughness and intransigence, left his beautiful lands in the Midi. With his face toward Jerusalem, his hope lay irrevocably in the ideal of service to his Lord. Goals today are different, but the dynamics of crusading remain the same.

JOHN HUGH HILL
LAURITA L. HILL

HOUSTON, TEXAS
March, 1962

PREFACE

IT IS A RENEWED honour for me to present the American edition of the work devoted to Raymond IV of St. Gilles by my friends Laurita and John Hill, after the French version published by Ed. Privat in 1959.

On the whole, the reception of the book by the critics was a very favourable one. It is only natural that some minor reservations should have been made. But, on the major issues, the agreement is fairly general. For Paul Rousset, "la forte personnalité de Raymond de St.-Gilles mérite la considération, et le livre des deux historiens americains vient réparer une injustice." (*Le Moyen Age,* 1961, no. 1–2, p. 177) Mlle. El. Magnou expresses the view that "plus que d'une réhabilitation enthousiaste, il s'agit ici d'une étude critique patiente, réfléchie, convaincante: oeuvre d'historiens de métier qui pratiquent avec aisance l'art difficile de lire les documents." (*Cahiers de Civilisation Médiévale,* Oct.–Dec. 1960, pp. 506–508) "They have produced a strikingly original account of the First Crusade and have also added materially to our critical appreciation of the sources for that expedition, especially Raymond d'Aguilers," says Mr. J. Gordon Rowe. (*Speculum,* July 1960, pp. 462–63) Prof. Loren C. McKinney has it "a well buttressed and generally convincing rehabilitation of Raymond's reputation." (*American Historical Review,* April 1960, pp. 656 ff.) Prof. Steven Runciman, whose works on the Crusade are well known, admits that "the authors . . . to some extent . . . succeed in making their point," although they "push their case a little too far." (*English Historical Review,* July 1961, pp. 515–16) More quotations

viii PREFACE

could be made. They would not alter this rejoicing impression of unanimity.

It should also be mentioned that this French version obtained in 1961 the "prix Albert Marfan" awarded every second year by the Académie des Jeux Floraux. This is the oldest Academy in Europe, its first manifestation being the invitation sent in 1323 by seven troubadours to all poets writing in the idiom of oc. For the first time a golden violet was awarded to a local poet on the third of May, 1324. Through the centuries, the Company of Gay Learning (Companhia del Gai Saber), then College of Rhetoric—to which Louis XIV gave the official status of an Academy—preserved and widened this tradition. Every year, on May 2 and 3, it distributes prizes and flowers. Their work, which combined erudite honesty with sympathy for their subject, designated Laurita and John Hill for one of its prizes in 1961.

My last words should express a wish. The present work rests mainly on a *critical* examination of the *Historia Francorum qui ceperunt Iherusalem,* by Raymond of Aguilers. Let us hope that Laurita and John Hill will soon be able to provide us with a *critical* edition of this text. This would be a new and precious contribution to a better knowledge of the Crusades.

PHILIPPE WOLFF

TOULOUSE, FRANCE
February, 1962

CONTENTS

RAYMOND IV
Count of Toulouse

THE HOUSE OF TOULOUSE

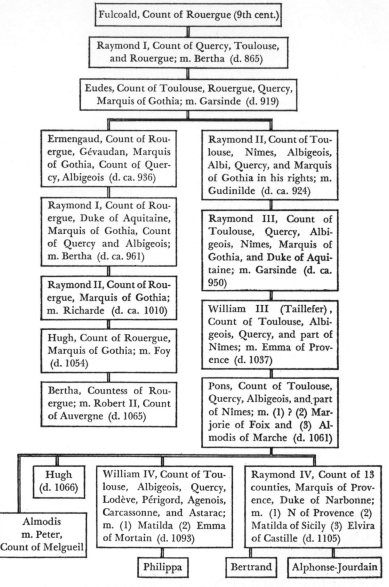

Fulcoald, Count of Rouergue (9th cent.)

Raymond I, Count of Quercy, Toulouse, and Rouergue; m. Bertha (d. 865)

Eudes, Count of Toulouse, Rouergue, Quercy, Marquis of Gothia; m. Garsinde (d. 919)

Ermengaud, Count of Rouergue, Gévaudan, Marquis of Gothia, Count of Quercy, Albigeois (d. ca. 936)

Raymond I, Count of Rouergue, Duke of Aquitaine, Marquis of Gothia, Count of Quercy and Albigeois; m. Bertha (d. ca. 961)

Raymond II, Count of Rouergue, Marquis of Gothia; m. Richarde (d. ca. 1010)

Hugh, Count of Rouergue, Marquis of Gothia; m. Foy (d. 1054)

Bertha, Countess of Rouergue; m. Robert II, Count of Auvergne (d. 1065)

Raymond II, Count of Toulouse, Nîmes, Albigeois, Albi, Quercy, and Marquis of Gothia in his rights; m. Gudinilde (d. ca. 924)

Raymond III, Count of Toulouse, Quercy, Albigeois, Nîmes, Marquis of Gothia, and Duke of Aquitaine; m. Garsinde (d. ca. 950)

William III (Taillefer), Count of Toulouse, Albigeois, Quercy, and part of Nîmes; m. Emma of Provence (d. 1037)

Pons, Count of Toulouse, Quercy, Albigeois, and part of Nîmes; m. (1) ? (2) Marjorie of Foix and (3) Almodis of Marche (d. 1061)

Hugh (d. 1066)

Almodis m. Peter, Count of Melgueil

William IV, Count of Toulouse, Albigeois, Quercy, Lodève, Périgord, Agenois, Carcassonne, and Astarac; m. (1) Matilda (2) Emma of Mortain (d. 1093)

Raymond IV, Count of 13 counties, Marquis of Provence, Duke of Narbonne; m. (1) N of Provence (2) Matilda of Sicily (3) Elvira of Castille (d. 1105)

Philippa

Bertrand

Alphonse-Jourdain

Raymond IV inherited the lands of his cousin, Bertha, when she died in 1065. This strengthened the line and settled the troublesome problem of divided rights.

IN LANGUEDOC

IN THE YEAR of our Lord 1096, Raymond of Saint-Gilles, most excellent leader of the Christian militia and dearest son of the Holy Roman church, knelt before the altar of the abbey of Chaise-Dieu. Here he prayed to his beloved Saint Robert for success in the greatest of his many quests. Once before Raymond had sought the intercession of his favorite saint in the solitude of the House of God, when ambition drove him to seek his paternal rights in the county of Toulouse.

Now an old man contemplating his gray hairs, as William of Malmesbury would have us believe, he was planning his last venture.[1] Months before, his emissaries had promised the Holy Father, Pope Urban II, that their master would take the Cross and lead his army to Jerusalem. Now, on bended knees, the un-crowned king of the Midi implored Saint Robert to aid him in his holy cause. Departing later from the cherished abbey of Chaise-Dieu, Raymond carried a talisman, the cup of Saint Robert, to guide him on his last journey. In his future lay the recovery of the Holy Sepulcher for Christendom and burial far from his native land; but the cup of Saint Robert would, at his request, be returned to rest once more within the lonely walls of Chaise-Dieu.[2]

Contemporaries, continuators, and critics would write many contradictory things concerning Raymond. We can read that he spent his life fighting neighboring lords as well as Moslems in Spain and the Near East. The first to take the watch at night and the last to leave, he was a soldier who struck the fancy of his pagan enemies. "Saint-Gilles, may God curse him," they wrote in their chronicles as they acknowledged his prowess. His fighting ventures cost him an eye and, later, Moslems state, his life in the flaming timbers of Mount Pilgrim, a haven for travelers to the Holy Land.[3] He is pictured often as greedy, superstitious, irascible, quick to anger, a man who had no desire for a legitimate wife, yet one who "shone amidst all the Latins 'as the sun amidst the stars of heaven.'" He was described as a man "commendable in all things, a valiant knight, and a devout servant of God." His greed and fanaticism are the subjects of facile pens of the twentieth century.[4] Merciless in combat, he ordered his men to cut off the hands and feet of his Slavic prisoners and to scatter their mutilated bodies on the mountainous trails as terrible reminders to their comrades.[5] Certainly, if Raymond deserved all that has been written of him, he represents the stern contrasts of the Middle Ages, the violence of holy war in the midst of sincere religious sentiment.

It is one thing to represent the Middle Ages. It is another to share the leadership of its most spectacular movement. What had there been to distinguish this lord of the Midi from any other petty nobleman born on European soil in the opening years of the fourth decade of the eleventh century? A younger son in a county drifting toward primogeniture, his prospects, like those of his uncle, Bertrand, Count of Venaissin, would ordinarily have included only the possession of some part of his mother's estate, and his history, the occasional occurrence of his name upon a dusty charter. Yet this man, now the uncrowned king of the Midi, was about to set out for Jerusalem with his stubbornness of purpose, an apparently unlimited purse, and the largest contingent of men on the crusade. His companion of the journey would be the pope's vicar, Adhémar, Bishop of Le Puy. Likened to Moses and Aaron, they would lead their people to the Holy Land.

No one could have known of these events when Almodis, daughter of Bernard, Count of the March in Limousin, in one of her many accouchements gave birth to her famous son. The date of his birth is uncertain, perhaps 1041 or 1042.[6] His land, Languedoc, was in the eleventh century the core of the Midi. Roughly bounded on the north by the valleys of the upper

Loire, on the west by the Garonne, on the south by the Pyrenees, and on the east by the Rhône, this land had been a thoroughfare where roamed Phoenicians, Greeks, Romans, Visigoths, Vandals, Burgundians, Syrians, Jews, Saracens, Hungarians, and Franks. Roads, aqueducts, crumbling arches and temples, and heterogeneous people remained to mark their passing. These people, the Provençals, wrote Ralph of Caen, "had a haughty look, a fierce spirit, and were prompt to spring to arms. They differed from other inhabitants of France as much as ducks from chickens. They lived on little and were known to eat roots." Even their youngsters sang, "The Franks to war, the Provençals to food." [7]

This Norman historian failed to note far more pertinent differences between the people of northern and southern France. Favored by existence of money and their closeness to the Mediterranean, the durable Provençals had recovered by the time of Raymond's birth from the more recent incursions of some of their barbaric neighbors and had established sufficient stability for trade. In this region one held his land not from symbolic ceremony but by virtue of written documents, and it was still possible to buy and sell land as a remedy for the inequalities resulting from the passage of time. The Peace of God and the Truce of God had taken hold in the Midi as in no other part of Europe, and the lords of the region could protect themselves and their possessions by mutual oaths of friendship and support. Traders, clergymen, and peasants found themselves more secure from armed bands. In such a land pilgrims had the leisure and comparative safety to view Roman ruins and the remains of cities sacked by Moslems as well as to contemplate the unintelligible inscriptions of antiquity. Traveling routes to the shrine of Saint James of Compostello, they found incentives to visit sacred places along the way in Languedoc.[8]

This comparative stability developed in the Midi in a century when England was to fall to the Normans, when the French king could not exact homage from his powerful vassals, and when the Holy Roman Empire and the papacy would disrupt the peace of Europe with their differences. Such stability could have existed only in the absence of severe outside pressures and in the presence of strong leadership within the country. For this guidance some would look to the house of Toulouse and to the provincial church. Frankish in origin, the counts of Toulouse can be traced from the ninth century. As palatine counts they held their lands directly from the French king. As powerful nobles they had become independent to the extent that they recognized their overlords only in the formulas of their charters. They had divided their lands among their sons until much of their rich patrimony was held by agnate heirs. Having reached the point where further division seemed impractical, Pons, Raymond's father, had inherited the county of Toulouse and other paternal lands. That he intended to continue this pattern of inheritance is indicated by a charter of Gauzebert, Abbot of Moissac, who acknowledged the confirmation of the union of the abbey of Moissac and Cluny in the presence of William, the young son of Pons. This charter indicates that if William left no male heirs, then the second brother, Raymond, was to inherit, and in turn if Raymond left no sons, then the third son, Hugh, was to fall heir to the patrimony.[9]

In his usual garrulous fashion, William of Malmesbury, writing years later, tells us that Pons was an energetic count descended from a long line of indolent ancestors.[10] However, incursions of Norsemen, Hungarians, and Saracens, to say nothing of inroads of the Frankish government, could have given the counts of Toulouse little time for indolence. Pons, son of William Taillefer, Count of Toulouse, and his second wife, Emma of Provence, was married three times. His marriage to Almodis, mother of Raymond, was the last of his matrimonial ventures. His life, apparently a turbulent one, was marked by conflicts with the church over usurpation of church lands. By 1061 he was dead, perhaps at the age of sixty-six. This stormy old count lay at rest in a tomb of white marble in the church of Saint-Sernin of Toulouse guarded by images of the Virgin, Saint Jacques, and Saint Sernin. His children continued to preserve his memory by making grants to the church, with the hope, perhaps, that his sins would be forgiven.[11]

Enjoying as he did unearthing or fabricating scandals in the house of Toulouse, William of Malmesbury wrote that Raymond's mother, Almodis, was a woman of "sad, unbridled lewdness." [12]

Certainly, within a few years she had married three times. After an unsuccessful marriage to Hugh of Lusignan, she was married to Pons, Count of Toulouse, in 1040. From this union came three sons and a daughter, Almodis. In 1053 or 1054 Raymond's mother abandoned Pons and married Raymond-Bérengar, Count of Barcelona, by whom she had twins, Raymond-Bérengar and Bérengar-Raymond. Some historians have conjectured that she was murdered by her stepson, Peter. We only know that she was dead by 1077 or 1078.[13] Actually, our thread of dependable information stems from the appearance of her name in the *Usatges* of Barcelona, where she is termed most wise, and in the charters of Languedoc and Barcelona. Yet from this we may conclude that she was an unsung but noteworthy ancestor of her more publicized descendant, Eleanor of Aquitaine.[14]

So William of Malmesbury would lead us to believe that Raymond's forebears were an illustrious stock given to the peccadillos of the time. As best we can piece together the fragments of charters and opinions of near contemporaries, the blood heritage of Raymond was vigorous, restless, and unpredictable. His youth presents us with the same problem of scant recordings. The first fifty years of his life could have been little different from those of any feudal lord of his time except for his marked success. William of Malmesbury further informs us that Raymond was much brighter than his older brother, William, who did not excel in arms.[15] The charters find him in his teens subscribing to a grant to Lézat in 1058 or 1060. He gave his title as Count of Saint-Gilles, the name he would make famous in Europe and the Levant. We are by no means certain of how he came by his claim to it. Historians conjecture that he was particularly devoted to Saint Gilles, whose shrine was in southern France; however, as an interest in the possessions of the abbey of Saint-Gilles was among the lands that Raymond was to inherit, it is more likely that his father conferred the title upon him, and that it carried few rights during the lifetime of Pons.[16]

Upon the death of Pons in 1061, the major share of the lands, the counties of Toulouse, Albigeois, Quercy, and possibly Lodève went to the pious and supposedly stupid eldest son, William IV. In view of the fact that William, as had his father before

him, inherited the paternal lands, there is little reason to credit
William of Malmesbury, who wrote that this count inherited
Toulouse because it would stir no opposition.[17] At the time of his
father's death, Raymond received a foothold in the Midi from
the dower lands. In 1037 Pons had given a dowry to his second
wife, Marjorie, and later to Almodis, one-half of the bishoprics of
Nîmes and Albi, one-half of the abbey of Saint-Gilles, the castle
of Tarascon, and the land of Argence. From this dowry William
received Albi. Raymond's succession included one-half of the
bishopric of Nîmes, one-half of the abbey of Saint-Gilles, the castle
of Tarascon, and the land of Argence. The youngest son Hugh
received no share, and was dead perhaps as early as 1066.[18]

From this humble beginning Raymond was to build his feudal
state in Languedoc within three decades. The ingredients of this
successful work appeared to be harmonious relations with the
Cluniacs and with the church in the main, fortunate marriage
and successions, and the occasional use of force. We catch a
glimpse of him in the abbey of Saint-Saturnin-sur-Rhône (today
Pont-Saint-Esprit), in the presence of monks, clerks, and laity, for
the good of his soul and the souls of his family, giving the abbey
of Goudargues to Hugh, Abbot of Cluny. In another act Raymond and his mother, Almodis, in 1066 subscribed to a grant
to the Congregation of Cluny by the abbey of Saint-Gilles. These
acts mark the beginning of a close association with the Cluniacs,
which lasted until Raymond went to the Holy Land. Unfortunately these charters leave us no information concerning the
influence of the Cluniacs upon the later crusading zeal of the
Count of Saint-Gilles, although writers have conjectured that
Raymond's understanding of holy war stemmed from the lessons
of the Congregation.[19]

Even as the counsel of the Cluniacs may be inferred in the
count's crusading career, so may their advice and support, or that
of other churchmen, be supposed in the events which are revealed
to us in this second charter concerning Cluny. In this grant Raymond assumed the title of the Count of Rouergue, Nîmes, and
Narbonne. This fortunate addition to his stature came as a result
of the death of his cousin, Bertha, a descendant of the younger
line of the family, which from the time of Ermengaud in the

tenth century had possessed the marquisate of Gothia (the counties of Narbonne, Agde, and Béziers), Uzès, and Rouergue. Bertha was survived by her husband, Robert, Count of Auvergne and Gévaudan, who sought to inherit her lands. Raymond, asserting family tradition, stepped into the succession, but he was not to have Rouergue without strife. The ensuing conflict lasted until 1079 and left Rouergue and Gévaudan desolated by war. Yet Raymond emerged victor with a claim also to Gévaudan; and through this military success, good counsel, and favorable opportunity, the family of Toulouse, whose lands had faced supporting two younger branches, now had only one to support.[20]

Although Raymond was to struggle long for Rouergue, by the year 1066 he had taken possession of the county of Narbonne. He made at that time an agreement with Guifred, Archbishop of Narbonne, in which he promised to aid this churchman against the bishops who blasphemed him, as well as to return to him some of his walls, towers, and fortresses in Narbonne. The count further agreed to give in fief one-third of what he received through the court of Narbonne to Guifred and assured him that the Viscount of Narbonne, Raymond-Bérengar, would let him enjoy his rights. This charter, which is one of several agreements with Guifred, an archbishop who is best known for his embracement of simony and his numerous clashes with the church hierarchy, leads us to believe that Raymond showed no interest early in his life in the reform movement of the church.[21]

Although we know from the subscription of his wife to the above charter of 1066 that Raymond was married, both the name of his wife and the names of her forebears have been lost. At least one historian has argued that this first wife of the Count of Saint-Gilles was the daughter of Raymond-Bérengar, Viscount of Narbonne, and Garsinde, daughter of Rangarde of the March, thus a cousin through Almodis, his mother.[22] However, such reasoning ignores the fact that, in addition to the lack of apparent territorial advantage in such a match, Raymond supported Guifred against this purported father of his first wife. Many historians accept the view on the premise of tradition in the Midi, that this wife was the daughter of his uncle Bertrand because her son was so named. Bertrand of Venaissin, who had lands from his mother, had not diminished family lands in his succession, and a marriage to his heir would be of considerable advantage to the Count of Saint-Gilles.[23] In either marriage he would encounter the laws of the church concerning consanguinity, and these had been evidently set aside by the provincial church, a matter which a high churchman could accomplish at a time when appeals to Rome were infrequent and the papacy was weak. In the Midi at this time the children of such unions were legitimate heirs to the estates involved, although the marriages themselves might later be dissolved.[24]

In this period of Raymond's life his mother, Almodis, continued to hold her family together with little regard for the county of Toulouse. In 1067 we find her in Toulouse confirming with her son, William, a grant to the abbey of Moissac. It is likely that her trip across the Pyrenees had been prompted by the marriage of her daughter, Almodis, to Peter, Count of Melgueil. Although no mention is made of the presence of Raymond, it is possible that she talked with both of her sons concerning the creating of an inheritance in Carcassonne for their half-brothers Raymond-Bérengar and Bérengar-Raymond.[25] Her influence prevailed, for in 1067 the Count of Saint-Gilles sold the abbey of Caunes to the count and countess of Barcelona, and they in turn agreed to give it in fief to Viscount Raymond-Bernard, capable head of the Trencavel family. Almodis continued to work to this end.[26] In 1071 Raymond was perhaps in Carcassonne as a witness to the sale of the castle of Laurac by his brother William to the count of Barcelona. Thus Almodis, even as Raymond worked to rebuild the fortunes of the family, contrived to sow the seed of its future weakening; because as Barcelona became a contestant for rights in Carcassonne, the powerful Trencavels, who actually held the county, played between the two rivals in a brilliant and strategic program of self-aggrandizement, which was to be terminated only by the Albigensian Crusade.[27]

A charter of 1070 between Raymond and Aycard, Archbishop of Arles, informs us that the young Count of Saint-Gilles was active by that time in pressing his interests in Provence. Raymond agreed to restore to Aycard the church of Saint-Paschal as well as lands which the church possessed in Argence, the third part of the castle of Foulques, and one-half of Albaron. He further promised Aycard one-half of the tolls upon the Rhône if recovered at Arles. Raymond's claims to part of Provence possibly came from his marriage to the heiress of Venaissin, Bertrand's daughter. Further addition to family lands arose through his grandmother Emma's inheritance. In the eleventh century the province belonged in common to the descendants of Rotbold of Arles and William of Avignon. The administration of Provence, however, was divided. Emma's son, Pons, the father of Raymond, had administered the lands of Argence, Tarascon, and the county of Die. Her son, Bertrand, had received Venaissin. Thus Provence, by recognizing cognate succession, was now partitioned among William, Raymond, their uncle Bertrand or his heir, and their cousins, the counts of Arles and Avignon.[28]

Other than witnessing a charter of his brother, William, while in Carcassonne in 1071, Raymond left no record of his activities for four years. Then, in 1074, we note the first clue that the papacy looked to Languedoc for aid from her enemies. On February 2 of this year Pope Gregory VII wrote to William, Count of Burgundy, praying that he head an army to relieve the church from Norman oppression, and thus execute his solemn promise, which he had made before the body of the sainted apostle, to aid the church. The pope further charged the count of Burgundy to instruct Raymond of Saint-Gilles, who had taken a similar oath, to march to his aid. They were to bring the Normans to task and then aid the Greeks against the Saracens. Other than this general statement of Gregory, there is no evidence that Raymond took this oath at Rome. We cannot assume, as have some historians, that he took the vow at a local church council. We can feel, however, that he did not answer the behest of the pope, for in October of 1074 a charter indicates his presence in the Midi, concurring with his brother in the union of the abbey of Figeac in Quercy to the Order of Cluny.

Perhaps because of Raymond's failure to answer the papal call, this papal good will, if we may interpret it as such, was of short duration. In 1076, in the Third Roman Council, the Count of Saint-Gilles was excommunicated on the charge of having contracted a marriage of consanguinity. The excommunication was ignored, and Raymond apparently did not abandon his wife at this time, a rebuff to the papal authority which no doubt gave rise to William of Malmesbury's later description, according the Count of Saint-Gilles the status of a man who had no desire for a legitimate wife. In this instance William, along with later generations, misunderstood or misinterpreted the position of provincial authority in its relations with the hierarchy of Rome. Pope Gregory could use the marriage as an excuse to enter into the affairs of the provincial church. Raymond, with the support of the provincial church, could ignore him.[29]

The ban on Raymond appeared to draw him closer to the simoniac Guifred, who likewise suffered from the papal wrath. In 1076 Raymond further guaranteed the archbishop rights in Narbonne. It was in this year also that William, the young lord of Montpellier, recognized the Count of Saint-Gilles as his suzerain and in turn received the promise of Raymond's aid in the defense of his possessions. Perhaps it was in this same year that Raymond witnessed, along with his brother, a grant made by Roger II, Count of Foix, in front of the abbey of Saint-Pons-de-Thomières. Thus with Raymond life went on, helped no doubt by the fact that Gregory was far away and busy. The house of Toulouse would work with the provincial church in matters of reform, and in its own good time rather than at the behest of Pope Gregory.[30]

Other difficulties arose, however, which could not be solved by accords with the provincial church. The countess of Barcelona, Raymond's mother, died. No act mentions her name after 1071; but in a grant made by the Count of Toulouse in 1077 or 1078, there is a strong inference that Almodis had died during the preceding year. Her death would mark the beginning of conflicts between Barcelona and Toulouse, and the families would be broken up in their play for influence in the lands which lay between them.[31]

Quicker was Raymond's resort to arms to restore harmony in another area. In 1077 or 1078 Stephen, Abbot of Conques, brought complaints against Bermond of Agde for the usurpation of the abbey rights. The dispute was submitted to a council of churchmen and laymen, and they returned a decision objectionable to Bermond. Raymond took the field against the usurper, ravaged his domains, and restored the rights of Palais to Stephen.[32]

Raymond, however, even as he acted in defense of the provincial clergy, was subjected to the displeasure of Rome once more. In November of 1078 Pope Gregory excommunicated him again. Raymond bore this ban along with his other troubles and continued to push for consolidation of his family's possessions. In 1079, perhaps through the intercession of Saint Gauzebert, the struggle for Rouergue came to an end. Apparently, the count of Gévaudan desisted in his pretensions to the lands of Bertha, and friendly relations were restored between Raymond and the surviving spouse of his cousin, the late countess of Rouergue.[33]

It was in this year of the settlement of the long struggle for Rouergue, 1079, that Raymond's friend of long standing, the Archbishop Guifred, died; and it is at this point that his first wife disappeared from the charters as mysteriously as she appeared. As with everything connected with her, there is no mention of her demise. Historians have generally assumed that she died at this time, although some advance the theory that Raymond abandoned her as a result of the second excommunication. We, however, can do no more than note, on evidence of the charters, that her signature as Raymond's wife appeared along with generous grants to Guifred, and evidence of her participation in Raymond's affairs disappears somewhere near the time of Guifred's death.[34]

This mysterious and controversial first wife of Raymond had left more to him than her lands. In the year 1080 the name of her son appears in the charters. At this time Raymond affirmed a grant of his brother, William, to the abbey of Saint-Pons-de-Thomières. William's grant, in addition to carrying the affirmation of his brother Raymond, carried the subscription of his nephew, the son of Raymond. This son, later known as Count Bertrand of Toulouse, was to be labeled as illegitimate by William of Malmesbury, and would bear the stigma until the twentieth century. This cleric of Malmesbury wrote, in his usual confusing way, that Bertrand was the son of one of Raymond's concubines. The count adopted him, so he informs us, because of a marked resemblance to himself. Guibert, writing in the twelfth century, following the papal excommunication of Raymond for a marriage of consanguinity, termed the son by this union a bastard.[35]

Followers of William of Malmesbury and of Guibert fail to note that Bertrand of Toulouse was regarded both by his family and by the provincial churchmen of his time as the legitimate heir to his father's possessions. Charters carry the name of Raymond's son as co-signer. Referred to as very noble in one charter, he bore the title of Count of Toulouse during his father's lifetime and during the lifetime of his half-brother, Alphonse-Jourdain. In the last charter which we have from Raymond, this son, Bertrand, as his father's successor, is charged along with the count's men and friends, to see that the bequest which the old count had made in favor of the church of Arles was upheld.[36]

In this same year, 1080, that we learn that Raymond had a son of sufficient age to witness charters, we also learn that he had contracted a second marriage. Perhaps mindful of former disapproval of a consanguineous marriage, Raymond went far afield for his second bride. Here fortunately, but perhaps not so dependably, we can turn from the desiccated pens of anonymous writers of charters to the words of Gaufredus Malaterra, who relates that Raymond's second choice was the beauteous Matilda, daughter of Count Roger of Sicily, thus the niece of Robert Guiscard and the cousin of Bohémond, a warrior and leader with whom Raymond would be later associated in the First Crusade.

Ambassadors were sent from Languedoc soliciting the hand of Roger's daughter, and after the usual amenities returned to the Count of Saint-Gilles loaded with gifts and Count Roger's consent. These niceties were appropriate to the rapprochement then current between Normans and Provençals. Raymond's brother, Count William of Toulouse, had married Emma of Mortain. Encouraged perhaps by his brother and by reports of his ambassador's, Raymond sailed to meet his prospective bride and in Sicily espoused her in the presence of the nobility and high clergy. Count Roger sent the bride and groom back to the Midi in a ship especially constructed for the trip. This charming picture, colored no doubt by Malaterra, leaves us uninformed upon a point of later interest. Did the Count of Saint-Gilles meet, during the festivities of his Norman wedding, his subsequent rival, his wife's cousin Bohémond, later Prince of Antioch? [37]

The trip to Sicily was but an interlude, and Raymond returned to Languedoc and his problems. Pope Gregory wrote him in 1081 in a friendly vein. The pope, in his renewed fight against simony in the Midi, was enlisting the aid of the powerful lords in a moderate program of reform. Guifred's death had not improved affairs in Narbonne. Guifred had spent the last decades of his life contesting the power of the viscounts of Narbonne, as well as incurring the wrath of the church. So now, despite the heritage of simony and civil strife, Gregory sought to fill the see of Narbonne with a devout churchman. This task was made doubly difficult because Bernard, Viscount of Narbonne, and his brother Peter had deprived Raymond-Bérengar of his rights in the county and had established Peter as archbishop of Narbonne. Gregory, in firmly opposing both this appointment and the continuation of simony, wrote to Raymond urging him to accept Dalmace, a man of pious life. The pope further suggested that he come to the aid of the church of Narbonne, which had become the prey of demons. Apparently forgetting Raymond's past support of Guifred and his previous consanguineous marriage, Gregory urged the Count of Saint-Gilles to resist "the usurper who had entered not as a shepherd but as a thief, sacrificing the lambs of God to give them to the demons." The count was to oppose this usurper with all force if he wished to obtain the Grace of God. He was to strive to propitiate Saint Peter, who would give him "goods in present and future life." We cannot say whether or not Raymond also forgot the past and came to the aid of Gregory. Certainly, it was not until 1086 that Dalmace came into the see of Narbonne, and no record remains of the influence of the Count of Saint-Gilles in resolving the differences.[38]

In the next several years, Raymond began to interest himself in reform. Whether influenced by Gregory or by provincial churchmen, the Count of Saint-Gilles subscribed to measures affecting various levels of the provincial church. Standing on the steps of the church of Saint-Nazaire in 1084, Raymond swore upon the missal to surrender the rights of possession of the inheritance of deceased bishops of Béziers. In return Bishop Matfred rewarded the count with a valuable horse. It was likewise at this period that Raymond urged the monks of Chaise-Dieu to reform the monastery of Saint-Bausile. In the next year Raymond confirmed all donations which the abbey of Saint-Pons-de-Thomières had received from Pons, his father. In the past Frotard, abbot of this ancient abbey, had been very successful in soliciting aid from his friends, William IV and his brother Raymond, Raymond-Bérengar, Count of Barcelona, and Sancho, King of Aragon and Navarre. In making the grant to Saint-Pons-de-Thomières, Raymond took the title of Count of Rouergue, Gévaudan, Nîmes, Agde, Béziers, Narbonne, and, although the charter is unreadable at this point, probably Uzès.[39]

Now as Raymond turned toward reform there occurred an event of great importance to him. Somewhere around the years 1085 or 1086 his niece Philippa, daughter of William IV of Toulouse and Emma of Mortain, married King Sancho of Aragon and Navarre. This marriage of William's sole heir, brilliant though it was, portends the decision in Toulouse to uphold male succession. Since the ninth century no stranger had administered the lands of the house of Toulouse, and there was precedent for brother to succeed brother in the absence of male issue. We can infer that Raymond's influence in the county was strong by this time. In only a decade he would be leaving it, never to return; yet in these after years, when Philippa would contest her patrimony with the heirs of Raymond, his name and his holy quest would be sufficient focus for a successful campaign against her.[40]

In 1086 Raymond was in Narbonne. He subscribed there with Dalmace, newly installed archbishop of Narbonne, to a grant to the abbey of Saint-Victor of Marseilles. This charter bespeaks an end to the old feud with the church over the see of Narbonne and reflects a trend toward better relations with the papacy.[41] Leaving this city in April, Raymond went to Saint-Gilles, where he welcomed his wife Matilda's sister Emma. King Philip of France, weary of his wife, hoped to marry this Norman heiress. But Emma's father, the shrewd Roger of Sicily, distrusting King Philip, sent his daughter to reside with his son-in-law while

negotiations continued. In such an atmosphere of suspicion, the
Norman master of the vessel which carried Emma's dowry sailed
from the Midi without leaving the treasure in Raymond's hands.
Raymond, having little regard for the wishes of the king of
France, subsequently married his sister-in-law to the young Count
Robert of Auvergne, son of his former rival and foe. From this
event we may infer that Raymond was yet living with his Norman
wife Matilda.[42]

After Raymond received Emma, it is quite possible that he
went from Saint-Gilles to southern Auvergne, an awe-inspiring
volcanic area, which has been described as a "vast, extinguished
conflagration." Shrine of Notre Dame du Puy, famed even in the
days of Charlemagne, Le Puy at this time boasted the chapel of
Saint-Michel, a quaint Romanesque structure perched at the top
of a peak, the Needle. Raymond's interest in the area stemmed
from his father. In extending his influence he laid claims to the
eastern parts of Velay, a land nominally divided between the
counts of Auvergne and the bishops of Le Puy. Here, in April
of 1087, Raymond met Adhémar, Bishop of Le Puy, a man of
"revered life." [43]

Earlier in the decade, having replaced the well known simoniac,
Stephen of Polignac, as bishop of Le Puy, Adhémar had continued to contest the power of the viscounts of Polignac. As a
fighting bishop whose abilities captured the interest of chroniclers, Adhémar had, according to some historians, just returned
from the Holy Land. Unfortunately, the nature of this meeting
of the Count of Saint-Gilles and the Bishop of Le Puy is obscure.
No mention is made of the conversation of these two who later
were to be leaders in the First Crusade. More capable of sub-
stantiation is Raymond's effort to extend his influence to possessions which belonged to the patrimony of the house of Toulouse.
This is evidenced by his subscription to an act in which Adhémar
gave the church of Usson to the abbey of Chaise-Dieu.[44]

In the following year, 1088, Raymond had returned to his lands
along the Rhône. He there made donations to the abbey of Saint-
Andrew of Avignon and subscribed himself as Count of Toulouse,
Duke of Narbonne, and Marquis of Provence. The titles revealed
here have led to questions of the proper dating of the charter.

As Duke of Narbonne, Raymond had, of course, revived the old
title of Duke of Septimania or Gothia, which had been possessed
by the younger branch of the family, whose last lineal descendant
had been Bertha. Raymond, had, however, changed the title to
Narbonne, metropolitan town of the province. The title of Marquis of Provence is not so easily explained. We are left to wonder
whether the title came from his father, from his first marriage,
or from the death of the last male heir in direct line in Provence,
Bernard of Arles. Subsequently, Raymond extended his authority
over upper and lower Provence and in 1089 settled a controversy
between Aldebert, Abbot of Lérins, and Richard, Abbot of Saint-
Victor of Marseilles.[45]

The assumption of the title of Count of Toulouse in 1088
presents yet another question. If the dating is correct, this title
was assumed while his brother William IV was still active in the
county and within a few years after his niece Philippa, William's
daughter, was married to Sancho of Aragon and Navarre. As we
have seen, there is evidence that he had begun to assume authority in his patrimony, as differentiated from his eastern holdings, which can be traced to dower lands and additions to the
family estate brought by his grandmother Emma of Provence.
In 1090, when he was approaching his fifties, we find him in the
seventh church council of Toulouse. In the presence of high
prelates he abandoned the rights of the abbey of Saint-Gilles
which his ancestors had usurped. This is one of several grants
which cemented friendly relations with the new pope, Urban II.[46]

Whatever our doubts of his bearing the title of Count of Toulouse in 1088 may be, by 1093 we can feel certain that Raymond
possessed the county. Two acts, however, signify that his brother
William still lived. Urban at this time gave William permission
to build a cemetery in Toulouse, and as Count of Toulouse William subscribed to a grant to Peter, Abbot of Sorèze. After this,
documents never mention his name. With such information
historians have inferred that this "very Christian" count undertook a pilgrimage to Jerusalem in the company of his half-brother
Bérengar-Raymond of Barcelona and died while on the journey.
William of Malmesbury relates that Philippa's father sold the
county of Toulouse to his brother some years before his death.

In this dearth of comment and conjecture we may return, if we wish, to the miracle of Saint Robert regarding Raymond's succession in Toulouse. According to this account Raymond, upon seeing himself deprived of his paternal possessions, went to the abbey of Chaise-Dieu and, accompanied only by a servant, entered the church and prayed before the tomb of the saint. Celebrating the mass of the great matin, Raymond paid homage to Saint Robert. Putting his sword above the altar, he swore that he would not hold the county of Toulouse if God did not intercede in his behalf. Proceeding then to Toulouse, he was accepted by the people. If there is any basis of fact in this miracle, we must infer that Raymond had gone a step further in his advocacy of agnate succession, which had served him so well in his eastern lands, and now pushed for the right of brothers to share in the patrimony, a right for which there was precedence in the history of the family.[47]

Close now to his crusading years, Raymond of Saint-Gilles, in his person as Marquis of Provence, on July 28, 1094, made important concessions to the abbey of Saint-Victor of Marseilles. In this document we learn that he had taken a third wife. Matilda, his former spouse, then was either forsaken or dead, and Elvira, daughter of a concubine of Alfonso VI, King of Leon and Castille, signed the agreement as the wife of Raymond. William of Malmesbury pretends that the marriage insured a covenant of peace between Raymond and Alfonso, although we have no evidence which points to difficulties between the two. Other historians have intimated that Alfonso rewarded the count for his services in defeating the Almoravides, pursuing the point so far as to suggest that Raymond fought in Spain in 1085, 1087, and 1089.

No eyewitness permits us to state that Raymond fought in Spain or lost an eye there, as is thus advanced. Raymond of Burgundy went to the aid of Alfonso, and confusion with his name may have led to the certainty with which some writers proclaim the Count of Saint-Gilles' role in the Spanish wars. It is plausible that Raymond learned to fight somewhere, and the petty punitive actions in Languedoc seem hardly a sufficient school in which to lesson a crusader of Raymond's combat stature. Following this logic a bit further, we can feel that opportunity for combat against the enemies of God was near by in Spain. Further than that we cannot go. Whether or not Elvira was a prize for such combat, we do not know; she was indeed a prize, as the nobility of her father would add to the stature and prestige of the house of Toulouse. By Spanish law this natural daughter transmitted the nobility of her father, Alfonso VI, to her children. We know that she accompanied her husband on the crusade and gave birth to one of his heirs.[48]

Soon after marrying Elvira, Raymond, "on contemplating his gray hairs, made a vow to go to Jerusalem, that his bodily powers, though decayed and feeble, might still, though late, enter into the service of God," or at least William of Malmesbury so explains the pious acts of Raymond from 1094 to 1096. However, we cannot feel that Raymond's dedication to crusading was quite so spontaneous. In less than two decades he had reversed his support of simony and had aided the reform clergy with grants and restorations of their usurped rights. In the eyes of Urban II he was "dilectus filius noster Raimundus." [49]

On September 1, 1094, before the altar of Saint-Gilles, Raymond, Elvira, and Bertrand renewed the abandonment of rights usurped by the counts of Toulouse. This reiteration of a concession made in 1090 to the abbey of Saint-Gilles was later taken cognizance of by Pope Urban at both the councils of Cremona and Piacenza. In 1095, again in the region of the Rhône, Raymond, Elvira, and Bertrand went to the abbey of Psalmodi in Nîmes and there upon the altar of Saint Peter surrendered many rights, reserved only a few, and received in payment two thousand sols of the money of Saint-Gilles. In June of the same year Bertrand married Helen of Burgundy and his father conceded to him holdings in Rouergue, Viviers, Digne, and Avignon.

This year, 1095, marks the apogee of Raymond's power in Languedoc. Rich, powerful, and proud, he now laid claim to thirteen counties—Toulouse, Cahors, Albi, Lodève, all newly secured from his brother, and Rouergue, Narbonne, Agde, Béziers, Nîmes, Uzès, Gévaudan, Viviers, and Venaissin, the aggregate of his older possessions. The Count of Die was a vassal and the Count of Foix recognized his suzerainty. His influence also extended into Velay and Provence. Yet it would be a mistake to exaggerate Raymond's power in the Midi upon the basis of the few charters that we have cited. The bonds which held Languedoc were loose, and much depended upon the friendship and counsel of his vassals. His was a leadership engendered perhaps by expediency and opportunism. With his prestige so acquired and with his respect for the law, he was able to weld Languedoc into the semblance of a state. Yet when he set out on the First Crusade, he had not overcome the problem of the two rival neighbors, William IX of Aquitaine and the count of Barcelona. When Raymond was absent on the crusade and Bertrand was administering Toulouse, his powerful vassals, the Trencavel family, would use these outside forces to their own advantage and to the detriment of Raymond's state.[50]

Yet, whatever the future held for Toulouse, we may feel that Raymond himself was in 1095 well ensconced in his holdings after a lifetime of patient restoration of the family possessions. Little different still from many another powerful lord, it is doubtful that these earlier efforts would have attracted a great body of historical interest. It was to be the next decade of his life that would imprint his deeds in the annals of history and the First Crusade. Perhaps the most controversial and enigmatic of all crusaders, he would first receive history's approval of his efforts. Later history would rob him of his just repute, and then again turn slowly toward re-evaluation of his achievements. This important decade would come to Raymond and to history as a result of a dream of Pope Urban II, who was even at this time on his way to southern France while Raymond, no doubt, was celebrating the marriage of his son to his noble bride, Helen of Burgundy.[51]

NOTES

1. Willelmus Malmesbiriensis, *De gestis regum Anglorum,* libri quinque in *Rerum Britannicarum Medii Aevi Scriptores,* II, 456 (hereafter cited William of Malmesbury).

2. *Acta sanctorum quotque toto orbe coluntur, vel a Catholicis scriptoribus celebrantur,* Aprilis III, 332 (hereafter cited *Acta Sanctorum*).

3. Abou'l-Fedâ, *Résumé de l'histoire des croisades* in *Recueil des historiens des croisades: historiens orientaux,* Vol. I, 9 (hereafter cited Abou'l-Fedâ in *RHC Or*); Raimundus de Aguilers, *Historia Francorum qui ceperunt Iherusalem* in *RHC Occ.,* III, 235–36 (hereafter cited Raymond d'Aguilers).

4. *The Alexiad of the Princess Anna Comnena,* p. 267 (hereafter cited, *The Alexiad*); Radulphus Cadomensis, *Gesta Tancredi in expeditione Hierosolymitana* in *RHC Occ.,* III, 617 (hereafter cited Ralph of Caen); Jacques de Vitry, *The History of Jerusalem,* p. 12. The inconsistencies of Raymond's crusading acts are often exaggerated by his chaplain, Raymond d'Aguilers, who at times uses Raymond as a subject for his allegorical and liturgical digressions. Failure to evaluate these passages has caused modern historians to heap reproaches upon the name of the Count of Saint-Gilles. Encomiums showered upon Raymond by his most bitter critic, Ralph of Caen, reveal that he understood that the accounts of the crusades became vehicles for didacticism. But one may read today that Raymond was "as pious as a monk and as land-greedy as a Norman."

5. Raymond d'Aguilers, pp. 235–36.

6. Devic (Dom. Cl.) et Vaissete (Dom. J.), *Histoire générale de Languedoc,* III, 339 and 565 (hereafter cited *HGL*). Unless further proof is offered, the exact date of Raymond's birth must remain conjectural.

7. Ralph of Caen in *RHC Occ.,* III, 651. L. Thibaux has noted in a review of the French edition of this work that the usage of the word Provençal is not accurate. This is true, but the usage follows the general classification used by the sources of the period. Certainly, Ralph of Caen's description represents a group image of people in the Midi rather than people in Provence. The same oversimplification of sectionalism lingers in the United States and has validity only in general terms. In this sense we use the word Provençals reluctantly. See L. Thibaux's review in *Provence Historique,* Tome X, Fascicule 39 (Janvier-Mars, 1960).

8. Loren C. MacKinney, "The People and Public Opinion in the Eleventh Century Peace Movement," *Speculum,* V, 1930; Y. Renouard, "Le pèlerinage à St. Jacques de Compostelle et son importance dans le monde médiéval," *Revue Historique,* CCVI (1951).

9. *HGL,* III, 297–99, 342; IV, 30–31, 191–95; V, 522. Interest in pressing *de jure* rights of the house of Toulouse is evident a genera-

tion before Raymond of Saint-Gilles. Charters of Pons, Count of Toulouse, cite him as palatine count with rights in Provence, Aquitaine, and perhaps Rouergue. Raymond was later to unite his holdings along similar lines and according to principles expressed in the phrase "every land according to its law." This principle resulted in agnate succession in the family lands and cognate succession in neighboring Provence, where Emma, Raymond's grandmother, had brought rights in half of the county.

10. William of Malmesbury, p. 455.

11. *HGL*, III, 338; V, 427, 502, 648–52; Joseph Calmette, "Les comtés et les comtes de Toulouse et de Rodez sous Charles le Chauve," *Annales du Midi*, XVII (1905), 5–26; Léonce Auzias, "Bernard 'Le Veau' et Bernard 'Plantevelue' comtes de Toulouse," *Annales du Midi*, XLIV, 603–13; René Pourpardin, *Le Royaume de Provence sous les Carolingiens (855–933)*, p. 233. See also J. Calmette in *Le monde féodal* for additional bibliography as well as files of *Annales du Midi*. The charters in *HGL*, V, offer the most reliable information.

12. William of Malmesbury, pp. 455–56.

13. *Chronicon Malleacense* in *Recueil des historiens des Gaules et de la France* (hereafter cited *RHGF*), Vol. XI, 219; *HGL*, III, 299, 338, 387–88; *Ex Gestis Comitum Barcinonensium*, in *RHGF*, XI, 289. Some historians cite the text of the penance of Peter for the murder of Almodis; however, Diago and others believed that she survived Peter. There is a donation to the abbey of Moissac on the fourteenth or fifteenth of March 1077 or 1078, in memory of the mother of William, Count of Toulouse.

14. Ramon d'Abadal i Vinyals et Ferràn Valls Taberner, editors, *Usatges de Barcelona*, p. 2.

15. William of Malmesbury, p. 456.

16. Jean de Jaurgain, *La Vasconie*, II, 301; *HGL*, V, 503–504. The dating of this charter in 1048 is apparently in error and is subject to the conjectural dating of 1058 or 1060. We believe that Raymond's devotion to the memory of Saint Gilles is exaggerated. Saint Robert seems to have been his favorite saint. The monastery of Saint-Gilles was the object of a pilgrimage as early as 988. See E. C. Jones, *Saint-Gilles*.

17. William of Malmesbury, p. 456.

18. *HGL*, III, 287, 338–39, 466; V, 428–29. We may assume that Raymond inherited his mother's dowry with the exception of Albi. The question of Hugh's inheritance and death remains obscure. Georges de Manteyer, *La Provence du premier au douzième siècle*, p. 308, argues

that Hugh received Die from his brother William and that, following Hugh's death, Raymond of Saint-Gilles possessed it and later gave it in fief to Isoard, Viscount of Gap. The authors of *HGL* as well as others have maintained that Hugh died without inheritance. The absence of Hugh's name in later charters does not support Manteyer.

19. The early grants to Cluny found in *HGL*, V, 531–32, 542–43, and 544, as well as later ones, form a pattern of great influence exerted by the Order over both William and Raymond. Unfortunately, we only know that Urban was on good terms with Cluny, that Cluny was influential in spreading the Christian cause at the expense of the Moslems, and that the counts of Toulouse were extremely generous to Cluny. We may only assume that Raymond's interest in the Holy War stemmed in part from the influence of Cluny. See A. C. Krey, "Urban's Crusade— Success or Failure," *American Historical Review*, LIII (1948), 235 (hereafter cited as *AHR*); A. Jeanroy, "Les troubadours en Espagne," *Annales du Midi*, XXVII–XXVIII (1915–1916), 157–59; Ernest Sackur, *Die Cluniacenser*, II, 302–303; L. M. Smith, *Cluny in the Eleventh and Twelfth Centuries*, pp. xxi–xxxiii; Prosper Boissonade, *Du nouveau sur la Chanson de Roland*, pp. 12–13. One of the greatest contributions of the Cluniacs was their leadership in the peace movement in the Midi. Fulcher of Chartres, one of the historians of the First Crusade, informs us that Urban called upon those present at Clermont to swear to uphold the Truce of God. See Fulcherius Carnotensis, *Historia Iherosolymitana Gesta Francorum Iherusalem Peregrinantium* in *RHC Occ.*, III, 323, 324.

20. *HGL*, III, 349–51, 397; V, 531–32.

21. *Ibid.*, V, 535–42.

22. Louis-André Vigneras in an unpublished dissertation on the life of Raymond has advanced the idea that Raymond married the daughter of the viscount of Narbonne and Gassinde, niece of Almodis and cousin of Raymond.

23. The long-accepted view that Raymond married the daughter of his uncle Bertrand has been advanced by *HGL*, III, 338, 387, 420, and by Jacques Flach, *Les origines de l'ancienne France, X^e et XIe siècles*, IV, 611.

24. This marriage took place long before Gregory VII's stand and almost a century before Gratian's *Concordia*, and at a time when there was a jurisprudence "coutumière" in each episcopal court. At such a court many considerations, legal and otherwise, would weaken the prohibitions concerning consanguinity—Germanic custom, Roman law (Justinian permitting first cousins to marry and Theodosian code per-

mitting by imperial indulgence), and economic pressure. Certainly, we do not contend that the canonical rules concerning consanguinity were not known before Gratian and applied as circumstances dictated. There is evidence that Raymond underwent a change of policy under the strong hand of Gregory VII. See A. Esmain, *Le mariage en droit canonique*, pp. 55, 56, 88, 337, 339. *Theodosian Code*, 3–10–1.

25. *HGL*, III, 351; V, pp. 544–46.

26. *HGL*, III, 363.

27. *HGL*, III, 374–75; V, 588–90.

28. *HGL*, III, 358; IV, 56–75; V, 584–85; Manteyer, *op. cit.*, pp. 305–306. The undivided character of Raymond's holdings in Provence leads to misunderstanding of his power there.

29. Gregory VII papa, *Registrum, Epistola* XLVI, in *MPL*, CXLVIII, 325–26; *Gallia Christiana*, I, Instr. 44; *HGL*, III, 383, 384, 387; IV, 197. We may infer from Gregory's letter that Raymond had been in Rome during the pontificate of Alexander II. That this marriage was sanctioned by the provincial church is intimated by the fact that Raymond's wife signed with her husband and the archbishop, *HGL*, V, 536. See note 24.

30. *HGL*, III, 389–90; V, 607–609, 624.

31. *HGL*, III, 387–89.

32. *HGL*, III, 397. We have little evidence that Raymond resorted to force in the building of his power. In these two cases of difficulty with Stephen of Conques and the count of Gévaudan, Raymond restored harmony which apparently lasted for years.

33. *HGL*, III, 397–98, 420.

34. *HGL*, III, 420, 428.

35. *HGL*, III, 428–74. See notes 11 and 12 to Chapter VII.

36. English and American scholars have in general accepted Bertrand's illegitimacy. Steven Runciman, *A History of the Crusades,* I, 160, repeats this view. Many misconceptions have arisen concerning this count. Failure to note the correction of the dating of a charter in F. M. Rosell, *Liber Feudorum Maior,* I, 4–5, has led to the erroneous belief that Bertrand promised fidelity to the king of Aragon in 1078. Failure to follow the charters has resulted in ignorance of Bertrand's legal status in his own lands, which recognized no superior law. He appears there as son of Raymond, a count, and nephew of William, a very noble man (betrothed to Helen of Burgundy, who was dowered, as was the custom, by her prospective husband with family lands), as Count of Toulouse during the lifetime of Raymond, and as successor so named by his father. That a great change occurred in attitudes

toward such matters in the course of following centuries is evidenced by comparison of codes. That it came too late to be a consideration in Bertrand's succession can be ascertained by following the charters. That Bertrand should be singled out to bear the stigma of illegitimacy while heirs to neighboring fiefs escaped suggests that he, as well as his father, was a victim of political propaganda. *Forum Judicum,* tr. S. P. Scott, III, viii. (Issue from incestuous marriages may inherit if there are no other heirs, and these children shall not be reproached); *Las Siete Partidas,* tr. S. P. Scott, VI, xiii, 10 (A person born of incest is not a natural son and cannot inherit except by grant of privilege from the king). The latter code was compiled a century after Gratian and did not acquire full force until 1505 (*Las Siete Partidas,* p. liii). Esmain, *op. cit.,* p. 31, notes on the basis of Philippe de Beaumanoir (*Coutumes de Beauvais,* XVIII, no. 578, p. 279) that succession still depended upon secular decisions even in questions of legitimacy. In pointing out that such marriages were sanctioned by usage, *HGL,* IV, 195–99, cites William IX of Aquitaine, Gaston of Béarn, and Raymond-Bérengar and Bérengar-Raymond of Barcelona as legitimate heirs from marriages which Gregory's councils could condemn. *HGL* further cites William of Tyre, 11.9 and 21.5, who regards Bertrand as the legitimate heir of Raymond. *HGL,* V, 652, 653, 738, 739, 766, 767, 791. See notes 24 and 29 above, and Röhricht, *Regesta regni Hierosolymitani* (MXCVII– MCCXCI), p. 8.

37. Gaufredus Malaterra, *Historia Sicula,* in *MPL,* CXLIX, 1167–68; *HGL,* III, 449–50.

38. Gregorius VII papa, *Registrum, Epistola* XVI, in *MPL,* CXLVIII, 589–90; *HGL,* III, 447–50.

39. *HGL,* III, 443; V, 685–87, 691, 697–98.

40. *HGL,* IV, 194. Alfred Richard, *Histoire des comtes de Poitou,* I, discusses the claims of Philippa at length. We believe with *HGL,* IV, 191–95, that English pretensions to Toulouse were without legitimate basis. It has already been suggested in note 9 above that Pons of Toulouse, Raymond's father, had outlined the pattern of succession in citing sons to inherit. In this it seemed that Toulouse concurred. Philippa's invasions of Toulouse were timed to suggest that she protested Bertrand's recognition as heir and later Alphonse-Jourdain's succession. As she failed on both occasions to gain recognition for her *de facto* occupation, it is to be supposed that she could not muster sufficient support, and decisions in both cases went against her. On agnate successions, apparently the principle upon which Toulouse decided its successions, see note 45 below.

41. *Gallia Christiana,* II, 701.

42. *HGL,* III, 447–50; Rodericus Toletanus archiepiscopus, *De Rebus Hispaniae,* in *RHGF,* XII, 381.

43. *HGL,* III, 450; IV, 88–89; V, 699.

44. We have taken issue with the traditional treatment of Adhémar. See John Hugh Hill and Laurita L. Hill, "Contemporary Accounts and the Later Reputation of Adhémar, Bishop of Le Puy," in *Medievalia et Humanistica,* IX (1955); also Louis Bréhier, "Adhémar de Monteil," in *Dictionnaire d'histoire et de géographie ecclésiastiques,* I, and *Dictionnaire de biographie française,* III. The eyewitnesses give us very few facts concerning the deeds of the bishop of Le Puy. Consequently, Adhémar will remain a shadowy figure, capable thereby of arousing the wishful admiration of those who believe that strong leadership could have united the Greeks and Latins. See J. A. Brundage, "Adhémar of Puy. The Bishop and His Critics," in *Speculum,* XXXIV (1959); Stephen Runciman's review in *The English Historical Review,* LXXVI (July, 1961); Hans Eberhard Mayer, "Zur Beurteilung Adhemars von Le Puy," in *Deutsches Archiv,* no. 2, 1960.

45. *HGL,* III, 451–56; V, 707–709; IV, 66–75; *Gallia Christiana,* III, 191. See Manteyer, *op. cit.,* pp. 305–306, for a discussion of Raymond's title of marquis. See above, note 9. As the title of Count or Marquis of Provence belonged to Emma's branch of the family as well as to their cousins of Arles and Avignon, there is no reason to think that the house of Toulouse could not bear the title during the lifetime of Bernard of Arles, assuming recognition of sufficient support, which Raymond evidently was able to secure.

46. William of Malmesbury holds that Raymond assumed the title of Count of Toulouse in 1088. Raymond could have borne this title in 1088 either as recognition that he had undivided rights with his brother there or as indicative of the fact that he was heir to the county and already active in its affairs. Raymond II (*HGL,* III, 85; V, 137–38) used the title of Count of Toulouse during the lifetime of his father, Eudes. *HGL,* III, 86, believes that Raymond II and Ermengaud divided some of their holdings in 918; V, 145 shows Raymond II and Ermengaud spoken of as counts of Narbonne. Some have suggested that William preferred the succession of his brother to that of his daughter's husband. See Flach, *op. cit.,* IV, 588–89, 613. However, we doubt that Philippa was seriously considered as an heir. As early as 1080 both Raymond and his son Bertrand were affirming (*firmavit*) a charter of William. The policy of urging agnate successions in lands subject to family domination was understood by Pons, note 9 above, and the choice of Philippa's

husband, Sancho of Aragon and Navarre, was hardly one calculated to be acceptable for dominion in Toulouse. A. Richard, *op. cit.*, II, 54–56, recognizes that patterns of succession varied even within large fiefs and that there was a tendency to pass the great fiefs to male heirs—the collateral in the absence of males in direct line. He also cites the voice of vassals in successions.

47. *HGL,* III, 464–66; V, 730; *Acta Sanctorum,* Aprilis III, 332, *HGL,* III, 467; IV, 30, 31, 61, 63, 191–95; V, 652.

48. *HGL,* III, 469–71; V, 731–33; William of Malmesbury, p. 456; Ernest Petit, "Croisades Bourguignonnes contre les Sarrasins d'Espagne au XIe siècle," in *Revue Historique,* XXX (1886), 267; P. Boissonade, *Du nouveau sur la Chanson de Roland,* pp. 33–35. M. Defourneaux, *Les Français en Espagne,* pp. 136–43. Petit has led to the tradition that Raymond fought in Spain. We are inclined to agree, but so far as we can determine there is no corroborative source. See John Hugh Hill and Laurita L. Hill, "Justification historique du titre de Raymond de Saint-Gilles: 'Christiane milicie excellentissimus princeps,'" in *Annales du Midi,* LXVI (1954), no. 2.

49. William of Malmesbury, p. 456; Urbanus II papa, *Epistolae et Privilegia,* in *MPL,* CLI, 399. Fliche has emphasized the tendency of Gregory to make papal vassals of Christian princes. He further notes the fact that Raymond and Gregory were on good terms. However, Fliche does not state that Raymond was a vassal. He prefers to use the term, soldier of St. Peter. We cannot believe that the relations of Gregory and Raymond were as friendly as were the relations of Urban and Raymond. Nothing in the legal documents would lead us to believe that Raymond became anyone's vassal. See Augustin Fliche, "La réforme grégorienne et la reconquête chrétienne (1057–1123)" in *Histoire de l'église depuis les origines jusqu'à nos jours,* p. 128.

50. Jaffé, *Regesta Pontificum Romanorum,* I, 676; *HGL,* III, 472–73; V, 734.

51. For a summation of this change see John Hugh Hill, "Raymond of Saint-Gilles in Urban's Plan of Greek and Latin Friendship," in *Speculum,* XXVI (April, 1951). This work was published at the same time that Steven Runciman's rather sympathetic treatment of Raymond appeared. See R. L. Johnson's review of Runciman's work in *Byzantinoslavica,* XII (1951).

II

LAUNCHING
THE FIRST CRUSADE

FOR WHATEVER it is worth, William of Malmesbury wrote that Raymond of Saint-Gilles and the bishop of Cahors persuaded Pope Urban to preach the crusade. Contemporary chroniclers, however, preoccupied with signs from heaven, did not sense the importance of the inception of the crusade and failed to leave a record for continuators. If we follow the movements of Urban before and immediately after his call at Clermont, we can feel it is possible that he journeyed to Gaul in 1095 with the knowledge or hope that the core of military aid for his program would come from Languedoc and the Count of Toulouse. Modern historians who accept the view that Urban had a well developed plan for crusading, must also accept the fact that the pope devoted most of his efforts to enlisting aid in the Midi and that Raymond was the first of the great lords to accept his summons.[1]

From the moment of Urban's appearance in southern France, his associations and itinerary suggest that he was furthering plans for the crusade. His early contacts were made with churchmen from the lands of the Midi, men who no doubt knew the Count of Toulouse. Accompanied by Daimbert, Archbishop of Pisa and later Patriarch of Jerusalem, Pope Urban arrived in Valence in the early part of August. Here he met Gontard, a close associate of Adhémar, Bishop of Le Puy; and shortly thereafter in Romans he supported the cause of Hugh, Bishop of Grenoble, against the claims of the archbishop of Vienne. Hugh had been prior of the abbey of Chaise-Dieu. On August 15, 1095, the pope met

Adhémar when he celebrated the Feast of the Assumption at
Notre Dame du Puy. At this time he sent letters summoning
churchmen to a council at Clermont on November 18 of that
year.[2]

The meeting in Le Puy has caused many conjectures. Fliche
has suggested that it was during the conversations with Adhémar
that the pope was assured the military support of Raymond of
Saint-Gilles. A legend of Cafaro reflects, as Chalandon has noted,
the popular belief that Urban planned the crusade at Le Puy.
Cafaro relates that Duke Godfrey, Raymond of Saint-Gilles, and
other notables met in Le Puy to discuss plans for conducting an
expedition to Jerusalem. William of Malmesbury, perhaps following current beliefs, wrote that Adhémar had persuaded Raymond to take the Cross. Michael the Syrian likewise connects
the incipient stage of the First Crusade with the Count of Toulouse. He states that Raymond had an eye snatched out in Jerusalem for his refusal to pay the Turks a tax. The doughty old
count, so he relates, carried his eyeball in his pocket as a grisly
reminder and thus stirred the citizens of Rome to go crusading.
Michael's legend probably reflects the Eastern respect for the
prowess of the Count of Saint-Gilles rather than knowledge of
his pre-crusading contacts with Urban.

The contradictions in these stories emphasize the obscurity
of events. Yet the stories reflect a popular belief that Adhémar
and Raymond were key figures in Urban's plans. Fliche's suggestion has some support in fact. Urban made a trip into the
heart of Raymond's territory before the Council of Clermont,
and Raymond was prepared through emissaries to take the Cross
shortly after Urban's call. This latter fact seems conclusive proof
that the Count of Saint-Gilles at least had foreknowledge of
Urban's summons to arms.[3]

In turning to the lands of the Count of Saint-Gilles before
his appeal at Clermont, Pope Urban went to Chaise-Dieu,
Monastier, Nîmes, and on September 1, 1095, celebrated the
Feast of Saint Gilles in the abbey of the saint. No mention is
made of a meeting of Urban and Raymond at this time; however,
we cannot rule out a conjecture. The area of Saint-Gilles was a
favorite residence of the Count of Toulouse, and it seems that
his numerous grants to the abbey of Saint-Gilles would have

made his presence at such an important occasion a possibility. Pope Urban remained at Saint-Gilles a week and settled differences between its abbot and the bishop of Nîmes. Urban then recrossed the Rhône, visited Tarascon, Avignon, Saint-Paul-Trois-Châteaux, and by following the valley of the Rhône, recrossed his path at Valence and went thence to Clermont. This swing into Languedoc at least suggests that Urban had received assurance from Raymond and from church leaders that his appeal for a crusade might be well received in the area.

Urban opened the Council of Clermont on November 18, 1095, and with the exception of his crusading appeal, devoted his time to church affairs—the enforcement of the Truce of God, ecclesiastical discipline, and reform. Languedoc was well represented among the churchmen who thronged to Clermont. In the group were Adhémar, Bishop of Le Puy, Godfrey, Bishop of Maguelonne, Bertrand, Bishop of Nîmes, Dalmace, Archbishop of Narbonne, Peter, Abbot of Aniane, Bertrand, Abbot of Mas-Grenier, Seguin, Abbot of Lézat, and possibly Bernard, Bishop of Lodève, and Matfred, Bishop of Béziers.[4]

On November 27 Pope Urban, after arousing his audience with accounts of Turkish atrocities and the sufferings of Christians in Jerusalem, made an appeal to western Christendom to recover the Holy Sepulcher. Crusaders would wear the Cross and in turn would receive as their reward remission of sin. Having completed his call, the pope awaited results in what now appears to have been a well rehearsed drama. Adhémar, Bishop of Le Puy, "vir vitae venerabilis," knelt before Urban and asked permission to participate in the crusade. Closely following Adhémar came William, Bishop of Orange, "vir vere religiosus ac timens Deum," and then a great number of other churchmen. The reception of Urban's speech, despite whatever previous assurances he may have received, must have exceeded his fondest dreams. Yet the pope was a realist, and he surely understood that it would take more than clergymen to storm the walls of Jerusalem.

The following day, one which Fliche thinks was far more important than the preceding, Urban chose "dearest brother Adhémar" as vicar of the expedition. Probably on the same day, November 28, 1095, ambassadors from Raymond of Saint-Gilles pledged the aid of their master in the First Crusade. If this date is correct, then there can be no question of Raymond's fore-knowledge of the contents of Urban's address. Even if Chalan-don's suggestion that the count's emissaries arrived on Decem-ber 1 is valid, the time element still indicates that the Count of Toulouse was included in the rehearsal for Clermont.

Thus Raymond's acceptance of the Cross does not appear as spontaneous as Baldric of Dol would have us to believe. As a cautious, calculating man, who had built a feudal kingdom in Languedoc through fifty years of perseverance, he fits better into the assumption based upon the timetable of events. Even the language of his messengers, as we glimpse it, seems to suggest an accord rather than a hasty declaration. He agreed to lead a large force, to give part of his wealth to those who had no goods, and to refuse neither aid nor counsel to those who wished to go on the expedition. Contemporary writers also attribute to him the oath never to return to his native land. Although they con-cede this high motive to other leaders, they may have had some basis for Raymond's purported declaration, as his latter acts bear out their testimony.[5]

Modern historians, perhaps following a suggestion of Chalan-don, have assumed that Urban's appointment of Adhémar as his vicar denied Raymond the leadership of the expedition; however, the choice of Adhémar, fortunate as it proved to be, reflected in no way upon the leadership of the Count of Toulouse. The figure of Aaron and Hur holding up the arms of Moses was by no means absent from the thinking and planning of mediaeval churchmen. Baldric of Dol expressed the relationship of church and lay elements in the expedition when he wrote of Adhémar and Raymond as Moses and Aaron, who would lead the Chris-tian armies to recover the Holy Sepulcher. Urban's appointment of Adhémar upheld the hierarchy of the church. His dependence upon Raymond of Saint-Gilles merely stressed the spiritual quality of the bishop of Le Puy's leadership which, it was to be hoped, could unite the divergent elements that would accept the call.[6]

After securing adequate support, both lay and ecclesiastical, for his expedition, Urban set the date for the departure of the crusading armies on the Feast of the Assumption, August 15, 1096. The pope then resumed his journey on December 2, 1095, and for several months he traveled through Aquitaine, Anjou, Maine, and Gascony. In the following year, on May 7, he entered Toulouse to complete the launching of the crusade in Raymond's lands. His stay in Toulouse was broken by a side excursion to Saint-Peter of Moissac, best known of the Cluniac monasteries in Languedoc, where he confirmed the privileges of the house. Upon his return to Toulouse from Moissac, Urban consecrated the church of Saint-Sernin on May 24, 1096. Scene of reform controversies, this newly rebuilt church attracted many high churchmen and also Raymond of Saint-Gilles, who announced at this event that the church was entirely free. Raymond's recorded words at Saint-Sernin on this occasion give us our first written account of the meeting of the pope and the Count of Saint-Gilles. They may have met before, and they may have discussed crusading problems at this meeting in the church of Saint-Sernin. It seems plausible that they would concern them-selves with the crusade, as the season for the departure of the armies was near at hand. Monkish pens, however, preoccupied with the rights and glories of their own church, failed to en-lighten us.

The papal route turned in the early part of June to southern Languedoc, where the pope visited Carcassonne, Alet, Saint-Pons-de-Thomières, Maguelonne, and Montpellier. On July 6, 1096, Urban was in Nîmes, where the Count of Saint-Gilles awaited him again. Here, during the first session of the Council of Nîmes, he dedicated the cathedral in the presence of Raymond and of church dignitaries including Godfrey, Bishop of Mague-lonne, Bertrand, Bishop of Nîmes, and Isarn, Bishop of Toulouse. Two days later, largely through the efforts of Raymond and Urban, the long-standing quarrel between the canons of Saint-Sernin of Toulouse and Bishop Isarn of Toulouse was settled. On the twelfth day of July, in the presence of the pope and council, Raymond ceded in favor of the abbey of Saint-Gilles all the rights and usages which he and his predecessors had enjoyed in Saint-Gilles. At this time he swore that he would make the expedition to Jerusalem, presumably as a public recognition of the previous announcement of his ambassadors at Clermont. So far as we have evidence, this is the first commitment to the crusade which the count made in person.

The Council of Nîmes was ended on the fourteenth of July, and from there the papal party moved to Saint-Gilles, where the altar of the new church was consecrated. Perhaps at this time Urban dispatched a letter to the Genoese requesting their aid. Chalandon and Fliche surmise that Raymond of Saint-Gilles requested Urban to send this letter soliciting the help of the Genoese in supplying the crusaders. As later events show that the Genoese were loyal to the Count of Toulouse, it is reasonable to suppose that the pope was following Raymond's practical suggestion in enlisting their aid.

From Saint-Gilles Urban made a leisurely return to Italy after an absence of a year devoted to stirring appeals for the recovery of the Holy Sepulcher. In so doing he left no indisputable proof of his objectives or plans for the First Crusade. If he crossed the Alps still undecided upon launching the expedition as some historians believe, his itinerary suggests that it was in the Midi that he found the courage to make his appeal at Clermont. His journey further indicates that the Count of Toulouse was pre-eminent in the papal design. Urban visited favorite abbeys of Raymond. The pope's presence at Cluniac monasteries intimates that the Black Monks, whose order had experienced the expansion of Christendom at the expense of the Moslems, furthered the crusading cause. In retrospect historians dwelt upon the miraculous appeal at Clermont and overlooked Urban's more prosaic efforts. These, centering as they did in Languedoc, are our most reliable evidence of Urban's choice of means for furthering his cause.[7]

Even as he must have planned with the Midi in mind, in returning to Italy he left there the more practical problems of the crusade. In less than a year from the papal appeal at Clermont, the soldiers of the Cross from Languedoc were ready to march. Prosperous conditions and a long period of relative peace no doubt made possible this creditable record. In view of the success of the First Crusade and the fiascoes of later movements, it is well to recognize the organization of this motley group.

Collectively, chroniclers spoke of the forces of Raymond as Provençals. Individually, recruits came from many areas—Burgundy, Auvergne, Gascony, Gothia—which do not suggest Provence to the modern reader, as well as from Provence. To their fellow crusaders, the forces of southern France were the Provençals; but to Moslems the Christian militia were Franks, regardless of their origin.

Historians have attempted unconvincingly to compute the number of soldiers who forsook their country and followed the Cross. Some historians have conjectured that the leaders of the Provençals had mustered a force of a hundred thousand. It is hazardous, however, to estimate the size of the Provençal army because of glaring contradictions in reports of eyewitness historians. We can be sure only that Raymond led the greatest number of followers in the *militia Christi*.

Other characteristics of this army are of importance to us if we are to escape the mistakes of historians who have concluded that Raymond was unpopular with his own men because he seldom controlled them. Actually, loose feudal ties with his own vassals, coupled with the use of warrior councils to decide important questions, left him little more than one among equals. Other leaders might or might not support his counsel. Contingents that followed him from Gascony, Velay, Limousin, and Poitou, as well as many lords from nearby lands, owed him no allegiance and might assert their independence whenever they so desired. In this group were Gaston IV, Viscount of Béarn, William Amanieu II of Albret, Peter and Pons of Fay, William Hugh and Francis Lambert, brothers of Adhémar of Le Puy, Guy, Gerald, and Gouffier of Lastours, Raymond, Viscount of Turenne, Achard of Montmerle, Geldemar Carpinel, William III, Count of Forez, and Farald of Thouars. On the other hand, many of the best known and most powerful of Raymond's vassals were conspicuously absent. His own followers included Isoard, Count of Die, Raimbaud of Orange, William V of Montpellier, Peter of Roaix, Raymond Pilet, Peter Raymond of Hautpoul, and William of Sabran. The viscounts of Narbonne and Toulouse remained at home as did the powerful Trencavels.[8]

Even as many of the laymen might support Raymond or desert

him at will, the churchmen who accompanied the Provençals were also at times embarrassing to his leadership. Raymond d'Aguilers, canon of Le Puy and self-styled chaplain of the count, has left the best account of their activities. The seculars far outnumbered the regulars and included Adhémar, Bishop of Le Puy, William, Bishop of Orange, Bernard of Valence, later Bishop of Artasium, the bishop of Apt, and a great number of priests. Best known of the regulars were abbots from monasteries which were recipients of grants from Raymond. In this group were Richard, Abbot of Saint-Victor of Marseilles, and Arbert, Prior of Chaise-Dieu. The churchmen as a whole, including Raymond d'Aguilers, understood poorly the problem of supply and the necessity of strategy. To them, all success resulted from the power of the miraculous hand of God. All ill fortune stemmed from the greed of their leaders and the sins of the army. Delays on the journey occasioned their criticism. They looked to Raymond to lead them as quickly as possible to Jerusalem, and they had little sympathy and much blame for him when he brought the army to a halt.

The Count of Saint-Gilles was likewise burdened with the poor, who looked to him for support, which he often gave them. They praised or carped as their worldly goods increased or decreased with the fortunes of war. Raymond d'Aguilers mentions their poverty, their rapaciousness, and their dependence upon the largess of his master. Other historians liked to write of the parsimonious and greedy Provençals who eviscerated dead Turks so that they might recover gold coins which their hapless enemies had swallowed. At times this group more nearly resembled the ill disciplined peasant army which had preceded and often jeopardized the crusading venture.

The women who followed the army also posed a problem. Some were the wives of crusaders. Elvira, wife of the Count of Toulouse, went with the army and, according to some, gave birth to Raymond's second heir, Alphonse-Jourdain, on the journey. Anticipating difficulty from women who might not have so good a reason for accompanying the crusade as did Elvira, wife of the Provençal leader, Isarn, the bishop of Toulouse, prohibited Emerie of Altejas from taking the Cross and setting in motion a woman's crusade. Camp followers could not be avoided, and these became the object of moral sermons and scapegoats for numerous disasters in the crusading camps. More unfortunately historically, chroniclers concerned themselves with these episodes to the detriment of data which modern historians would classify as pertinent to crusading.[9]

Financial preparations for the journey are poorly recorded. The task of raising the money, equipping, and supplying the Provençals must have involved months of work. No doubt the lay leaders assumed responsibility in this matter for their contingents. Yet many lay leaders were of limited means, and the greatest burden of finance fell to the Count of Toulouse, if we may believe his contemporaries, who, without exception, wrote of him as the wealthiest of the crusaders. To these contemporaries, his method of raising money seemed of little importance. Robert the Monk merely states that he sold all of his goods before going crusading, perhaps reflecting the idea that the old count planned to end his days in the Holy Land. So far as records show, however, Raymond made few grants and sold but a small number of rights before his departure.

Inference may supplement the records to some extent. Geoffrey of Vigeois made a statement which has led some historians to believe that Raymond engaged a part of Rouergue to Richard of Millau, Viscount of Carlat. Some historians accept this reasoning with reservation and suggest that Bertrand alienated the land and instructed the Genoese to deliver the money to his father, who had departed on the crusade. Later transactions of the counts of Toulouse strongly indicate, however, that their forebears did not alienate Rouergue or other of their holdings. Rights of coinage, tolls on commerce in southern France, and other revenues due as a result of their dominion, comprised a fortune. The Jews of the Midi may have been forced to give aid, and most assuredly the church assisted in the raising of money.

Before his departure in the fall of 1096, Raymond may have added to his funds as he performed acts of piety. As we have noted, he visited Chaise-Dieu and persuaded its prior to accompany him. Perhaps at the same time he gave the abbey the

churches of Saint-Pasque le Vierge and Saint-Nazaire de Beau-
caire, as well as rights in Argence. Soon after, in the cathedral
of Le Puy before the image of the Virgin and in the presence of
the clergy, Raymond ceded to the church the towns of Segrier,
Bruguières, and Fabrejargues, with the provision that after his
death candles should be burned and prayers recited for his soul.
While in the neighborhood, he further surrendered certain rights
recently recovered from a rebellious vassal to the bishop of
Uzès. In addition he journeyed to Saint-Gilles, where once
again he officially recognized previously granted rights.[10]

In military preparations the Provençals had no recorder. By
inference their services of supply were good, for they successfully
crossed Sclavonia without suffering from hunger in these perilous
Slavic badlands. We can pick up the information as we read that
the principal forces of the army consisted of heavily armed
knights on horseback with helmet, cuirass, shield, sword, and
lance. The footmen were armed with bows and arrows. Elsewhere, behavior or colorful insignia caught the attention of
chroniclers. The foot soldiers were undependable because of
their love of pillaging. Albert of Aachen tells of multi-colored
banners of gold, green, and red among the knights. The anonymous author of the *Gesta* relates that Raymond's men were armed
on all sides with the sign of the Cross. Elsewhere we learn of
Raymond's seal, which was patterned after the Cross of Con-
stantine, and we hear of the Cross of Toulouse, which became
well known on many battlefields. The count's followers cried
"Tolosa!" as they placed their banners upon the enemy ramparts,
a feat made easier or frequently even possible because of Raymond's success in enlisting mechanics who could build siege
weapons.[11]

Recorded or unrecorded, these preparations took months, and
the army of the Provençals was one of the last crusading forces
to march. Although August 15, 1096, was the date set for departure, we feel reasonably sure that the Provençals did not
leave until later. No source states when Raymond and the bishop
of Le Puy quit the Midi. Fulcher, the only eyewitness to aid us,
states that all armies left in the months of April through October.
Scholars have made various surmises, and dates have been sug-

gested from August 15 to the end of October, 1096. However, if we believe that Raymond was in the abbey of Chaise-Dieu in October, as is maintained by some historians, then it is likely that crusaders from the Midi left toward the end of that month. The journey from southern France to Constantinople was not completed until the latter part of April, 1097; so this time element plus information on climatic conditions during the march of almost forty days through Sclavonia would indicate that Raymond's army started their journey in September or October. It is probable that the army did not leave in one large group, and that small contingents crossed northern Italy as a vanguard. Raymond was perhaps among the last to leave, as the chaplain, Raymond d'Aguilers, places him at the rear of the army in the march through Sclavonia, protecting his forces ahead from the harrying bands of Slavs and defending the stragglers, the sick, and the weak.[12]

So the Count of Saint-Gilles, wealthiest and oldest of the crusaders, now in his fifties, abandoned his native land, accompanied by his wife Elvira, the papal vicegerent, and a host of knights, footmen, bishops, priests, women, and beggars, all of whom were classified by Fulcher of Chartres as Goths and Gascons, and by other chroniclers as Provençals. When they were united by unified action with their brothers from the north, they were sometimes referred to as *Francigenae* by the Moslems who heard them shouting, "Exsurge Domine, adjuva nos."

The motivating force which placed Raymond at the head of this heterogeneous *militia Christi* remains today as enigmatic as upon the day of his ambassadors' appearance at Clermont. His contemporaries were satisfied to explain his acceptance of crusading as a manifestation of his sincere interest in the cause of the Lord. They criticized him upon occasion, but they accepted his sincerity of purpose. Nineteenth and twentieth century historians, under the aegis of material causation, have suggested that Raymond in his mid-fifties was seized with an insatiable desire for new lands and wealth. Perhaps through confusing the homiletic use of *avaritia* with a modern view of imperialism, they have come to view him as a man consumed with ambition to carve a new world for himself in the Near

East. In this they have overlooked what he sacrificed in leaving the Midi. Only Bertrand remained to protect his possessions. But Bertrand, as events would prove, was no match for William IX of Aquitaine. Even though Raymond might have hoped that Pope Urban's pledge to safeguard the possessions of the soldiers of the Cross would protect his lands, he certainly must have realized that death in a foreign land might well be his lot. In an age of religious sensibility, it is probable that Raymond wished to serve the Lord rather than to gain new estates in this world. But, as in all generations, his religious motivation became intertwined with practical politics.[13]

NOTES

1. William of Malmesbury, p. 456; Bernard Leib, *Rome, Kiev et Byzance à la fin de XIe siècle,* p. 15; Frederick Duncalf, "The Pope's Plan for the First Crusade," in *The Crusades and other Historical Essays,* pp. 47–48; Walter Norden, *Das Papsttum und Byzanz,* p. 49. For other works see A. C. Krey, "Urban's Crusade—Success or Failure," *AHR,* LIII (1948); C. Erdmann, *Die Entstehung des Kreuzzugsgedankens;* Alphandéry, P., et Dupront, A., *La chrétienté et l'idée de croisade;* P. Rousset, *Les Origines et les caractères de la première croisade;* M. Villey, *La Croisade: Essai sur la formation d'une théorie juridique;* M. W. Baldwin, "Some Recent Interpretations of Pope Urban's Eastern Policy," *The Catholic Historical Review,* XXV (1940). For an excellent summary of literature on the papal plan see Duncalf's footnote, p. 221, in *A History of the Crusades.*

2. See René Crozet, "Le voyage d'Urbain II et ses négociations avec de clergé de France (1095–1096)," in *Revue Historique,* CLXXIX (1937); also "Le voyage d'Urbain II en France," in *Annales du Midi,* XLIX (1937).

3. A. Fliche, *L'Europe occidentale de 888–1125,* p. 557; William of Malmesbury, p. 457; Cafarus, *De liberatione civitatum Orientis liber,* in *RHC Occ.,* V, 48–49; *Extrait de la chronique de Michel le Syrien,* in *RHC Arm.,* I, 327.

4. D. C. Munro, "The Speech of Pope Urban II at Clermont, 1095,"

in *AHR*, XI (1906), 231–42; Paul Rousset, *Les origines et les caractères de la première croisade,* p. 58.

5. Ferdinand Chalandon, *Histoire de la première croisade jusqu'à l'élection de Godefroi de Bouillon,* p. 46; Baldricus Dolensis, *Historia Jerosolimitana* in *RHC Occ.,* IV, 16. Michael the Syrian, *Extrait de la chronique de Matthieu d'Edesse* in *RHC Arm.,* I, p. 331. Michael states that Godfrey swore never to return.

6. Chalandon, *op. cit.,* pp. 48–49; René Grousset, *Histoire des croisades et du royaume franc de Jérusalem,* I, 4; Baldricus, *op. cit.,* p. 16.

7. *HGL*, III, 485–88; V, 742–45; Grousset, *op. cit.,* I, 5; Fliche, *op. cit.,* II, 560; Chalandon, *op. cit.,* p. 54; Cafarus, *op. cit.,* p. 49; Giuseppe Canale, *Neuova Istoria della republica di Genova,* I, 99–108, 352–53.

8. Guibertus Novigentus, *Historia quae dicitur Gesta Dei per Francos,* in *RHC Occ.,* IV, 150; Ralph of Caen, *op. cit.,* p. 629; *HGL*, III, 492; IV, 204; Raimundus de Aguilers, *Historia Francorum qui ceperunt Iherusalem,* in *RHC Occ.,* III, 244.

9. *HGL*, III, 484, 492; V, 757; Raymond d'Aguilers, *op. cit.,* p. 270; W. Porges, "The Clergy, the Poor, and the Non-Combatants on the First Crusade," in *Speculum,* XXI (1946), 10–11.

10. Robertus Monachus, *Historia Hierosolymitana,* in *RHC Occ.,* III, 739; Jean-Pierre Papon, *Histoire générale de Provence,* II, 538; Gaufredus de Briul, *Chronicon Lemovicense,* in *RHGF,* XII, 428; *HGL,* III, 490–91; V, 744–48; Jacques Bousquet, "La donation de Ségur par Raymond de Saint-Gilles, Comte de Toulouse, à l'Eglise du Puy en Velay (1096)," *Annales du Midi,* 1962 no. 1, 65–70.

11. Albertus Aquensis, *Historia Hierosolymitana,* in *RHC Occ.,* IV, 319; *HGL,* III, 493; Charles du Fresne du Cange, *Glossarium mediae et infimae Latinitatis,* V, 496, 498, and Typus num. 73. We have repeated the legend of Raymond's seal, although evidence for such is conjectural; Raymond d'Aguilers, *op. cit.,* p. 237.

12. Fulcherius Carnotensis, *Historia Iherosolimitana Gesta Francorum Iherusalem Peregrinantium,* in *RHC Occ.,* III, 327; Reinhold Röhricht, *Geschichte des ersten Kreuzzüges,* p. 76; Chalandon, *op. cit.,* p. 137.

13. The contribution of the Count of Saint-Gilles has been clouded by critics who attach undue importance to Raymond d'Aguilers' occasional criticism in which this cleric lapses into introspective episodes suggestive of homiletic *exempla*. In charging Raymond with *avaritia* during the siege of Antioch, the chaplain's general purpose is to cite the count as an inspiring example of great courage and a savior of the army; but in his brief introduction he places this warrior in a milieu

of mortal sin: ". . . comes praeter suorum voluntatem, castri custodiam arripuit, simul ut desidiam et avaritiam excusaret, et vigoris atque prudentiae semitam torpentibus demonstraret. Namque tempore praeteritae aestatis, gravi ac diuturno morbo fatigatus, et adeo mollis per totam hyemen fuerat ut nec ad militandum, nec ad largiendum promptus esse diceretur, et licet multa, quia plura posse credebatur, nullus esse clamabatur. Igitur nactus hanc difficultatem, scilicet materiam virtutis, tantam omnium invidiam passus est ut pene a suis privatis dissociaretur." To conclude, the chaplain remarks that as a result of vigorous action, "igitur invidia quam comes pertulerat, adeo lenita est. . . ." In this context, suggestive as it is of patristic disquisition—sin, its remedy, and the activity demanded of the soldier of Christ—even the illness of the count is suspect. See such expositions as Saint Ambrose, "In Psalmum primum enarratio," in *MPL*, XIV, 973–78 (avaritia morbos excitat"; "cave igitur ab impiorum consiliis"; "miles . . . stat, non sedit"); and "Liber de elia et jejunio" in *MPL*, XIV, 739 ("Jejunium . . . est . . . lenitatis institutio"); and Appendix, *Breviarum Romanum, pars autumnalis*, p. 8 ("Vincam . . . avaritiam largitate, iracundiam lenitate. . . . Redde me prudentem in consiliis. . . .") Fliche, *op. cit.*, p. 568; Raymond d'Aguilers, *op. cit.*, p. 250.

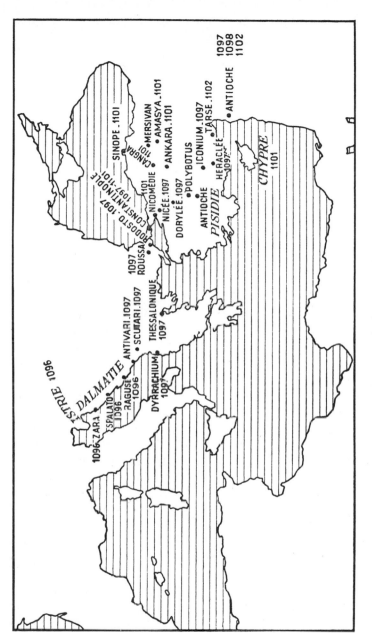

Itinerary of First Crusade

III

THE PROVENÇAL-GREEK
ALLIANCE

As the Provençals turned their faces toward the East, they felt that they would find friends and allies at Constantinople, whose ruler would assist them against the Turks, abominable infidels who now held the Holy Sepulcher in Jerusalem. The trip through northern Italy must have been uneventful, for no eyewitness mentions it. William of Tyre years later relates that the Provençals went into Italy, crossed Lombardy, journeyed through Forum Julii into Istria near Aquileia, and so came to Dalmatia, the Sclavonia of the chroniclers. Modern scholars, reconstructing Raymond's route, believe that the crusaders went through Lyons, Mont Genèvre, Lombardy, Milan, Istria, where they stopped at Aquileia, and thence into Dalmatia and the Slavic lands. Anna Comnena, daughter of the Emperor Alexius and author of the *Alexiad,* has puzzled historians by speaking of a count of Provence who engaged the Greeks in a sea battle after setting sail from the shores of the straits of Lombardy in a pirate vessel. As Anna habitually referred to the Count of Toulouse as Saint-Gilles rather than the Count of Provence, we may feel that she was writing of someone else, since Raymond was placed by his chaplain defending the march of the Provençals, a group so large as to make transportation by sea impractical.[1]

Entering Sclavonia, the Provençals traveled by the sea coast towns of Zara, Spalato, Antivari, and Ragusa. William of Tyre tells us that the people of the coastal region spoke Latin, so perhaps this kinship in language was a factor in their choice of keeping as close as possible to the coastal regions, as well as Raymond's dislike of putting himself beyond the reach of sea communications and supplies when in alien lands. Bodin, King of the Slavs, had enlarged his kingdom at the expense of the Greeks, and his people recognized the antipope Guibert. The Provençals, as followers of Urban II, could expect little friendship in the area.[2]

The count's chaplain has left a long lament of the painful journey across Sclavonia. Neither wild animal nor bird broke the monotony of this forsaken land. Dense fog and forests concealed the movements of the rude Slavs, ever anxious to strike the old and the sick, who could not keep pace with the army. To the chaplain it must have seemed a penance to prepare them for the glories to come. Citing the number forty, even as in the Flood, in the wandering of the Israelites, and in Lent, Raymond d'Aguilers relates that for almost forty days they struggled through the unfriendly land. Turning from his patristically tinged description of this perilous region, he gives us the first pen picture of the Count of Saint-Gilles.

We should not, remarks Raymond d'Aguilers at this point, overlook a certain glorious deed of the count, a leader who had been indefatigable in protecting the rear with its contingents of pilgrims. These duties kept him often from his tent until midnight or even until the cock's crow. The chaplain then reveals the mixture of cruelty and practicality in the count's character in his treatment of the Slavs. Finding himself and his few followers surrounded by the enemy, the Count of Saint-Gilles ordered a rush upon the enemy and seized some six of them. Then, fearful of counterattack, the count commanded his men to snatch out the eyes or sever the feet and hands of his tormentors and leave these hapless victims as bloody reminders of his power. At this point, Raymond d'Aguilers again becomes preoccupied with the mysterious ways of God, and we are left without further description of Raymond.[3]

As supplies began to dwindle, the crusaders negotiated a treaty of amity with Bodin at Scutari in January 1097. Influenced by the military might of the crusaders and promises of gifts, the Slavic prince promised to supply a market and provisions to the Provençals; however, depredations by his people continued despite the accord. In such unhappy circumstances, the Provençals welcomed with relief their entry into Greek territory. Even though their crossing of Dalmatia had resulted in no deaths either from starvation or battle (due, the chaplain tells us, to God's mercy, the toil of the count, and the counsel of the bishop), they rejoiced in the sight of Durazzo. The Greek governor, John Comnenus, a nephew of the Greek emperor, welcomed them, and Raymond d'Aguilers wrote that the Latins now felt that all was well because they were with their Greek brothers.[4]

In their elation at being among supposedly friendly people, the forces of Raymond of Toulouse did not take into account the crusading bands that had gone before them and their possible skirmishes with the Greeks. Certainly, Emperor Alexius was neither surprised nor unprepared. His daughter, the Princess Anna Comnena, writing years later, described the fears of her father as the host of warriors and unarmed pilgrims, "more numerous than the sand or the stars," approached his lands. William of Tyre likewise confirms the preparations of the emperor. Thus we can feel that the Latins posed a threat to the Greeks. The emperor, through his representatives, sent greetings and praise to Raymond, requested the Provençals to refrain from pillaging the countryside, and promised, perhaps in line with his understanding with Pope Urban, a market for the crusaders. With such assurances they departed from Durazzo after a short sojourn, leaving behind them William Hugh, brother of Adhémar, to recuperate from illness.[5]

Along the Via Egnatia Raymond d'Aguilers reports letters of friendship arriving from Alexius, but to the Provençals these were empty phrases because before and behind them, to the right and to the left, rode the imperial escort of the Turks, Kumans, Pechenegs, Uzes, and Bulgars. Ill disciplined and restless, the forces of the count clashed with the imperials, who, in the words of the chaplain, in the violent manner of lions attacked peaceful and defenseless Latins. In the ensuing clashes two noble knights, Pontius Rainaud and his brother Peter, were lost. Nevertheless, the Provençals resumed their march without incident, guided, as their chronicler states, by Christian love. But coming events would strain both the emperor's letter of filiation and the chaplain's confidence in brotherly love. They crossed the Epirus without further incident and entered the valley of Pelagonia in the middle of February, 1097. The growing ill will was heightened by an incident with the Pechenegs. In the neighborhood of Ochrida a group of them seized Adhémar, threw him from his mule, and would have killed him had not one of their number stood off his murderous comrades until help arrived.

Opportunity for revenge came toward the end of February. Beset by treachery of Alexius' troops, the Count of Toulouse learned that the Pechenegs were planning to attack his men from ambush in the defiles of a mountain near an unidentified castle named Bucinat. With this knowledge he was able to rout his would-be attackers. On the heels of this encounter there came new letters of welcome from the basileus, although, the canon of Le Puy remarks realistically, they were surrounded on all sides by the enemy and the guile of the emperor. In these troubled circumstances, the army lost the counsel and the strengthening presence of the bishop of Le Puy. Apparently he fell ill, perhaps because of injuries suffered at the hands of the Pechenegs. He was later to rejoin the army in its encampment before Constantinople along with his brother. At this point we have information which leads us to wonder if the skirmishes of the Provençals and the Greeks were not exaggerated by Raymond d'Aguilers to justify later events. Certainly, the freedom of movement of Adhémar and his brother, without the protection of the army, speaks for the efforts of Alexius to provide safe escort for the Provençals.

Likewise, we know that the precautions of Alexius were justified. The Provençals attacked the town of Roussa on April 12, 1097, and the fears of the emperor were realized. The chaplain offers no motive for the attack other than that it became evident the townspeople wished to make trouble and the crusaders lost their patience. The hungry crusaders, no doubt seeking booty as well as food, overthrew the ramparts, placed their banner over the town, and shouted "Tolosa!" Proceeding then from Roussa, they marched to Rodosto, an imperial city some four days' journey from Constantinople. Once again a skirmish ensued.

Once again a few imperial guards died, and there was booty for the Provençals.[6]

In the midst of these incidents on April 18, 1097, ambassadors from the basileus met with Raymond at Rodosto and requested that he travel ahead of his army so that he could confer with Alexius. Provençal envoys who had preceded the main army now returned to Raymond with the imperial delegation. The inference is that, on a higher level and unknown or unintelligible to the count's chronicler, crusading affairs at Constantinople demanded the presence and influence of the count. The count of Flanders, Bohémond, and Duke Godfrey were already there, and from other sources we know that their relations with the emperor were strained. Expecting an ally at Constantinople, they found an uneasy emperor, who demanded their homage. The disappointment of their men at this turn of affairs is reflected in the *Gesta,* where the author can reconcile himself only with the thought of their helplessness.[7]

Much to the disgust of his chaplain, the Count of Saint-Gilles determined to leave his army and hasten unarmed to Constantinople. The ensuing events made the choleric Raymond d'Aguilers even more bitter against the Greeks, for shortly after the departure of the Count of Toulouse, another fight broke loose between Greeks and Latins, probably on April 20, 1097. This event, which was to endanger negotiations at Constantinople when news of it came to Raymond, is so poorly recorded that we are left to wonder if the chaplain of the count was with the army at the time. After relating that the army was in despair and that some illustrious men had died, he instructs those "who wish to know of such details" to seek "from others more than from us." Apparently the Provençals were again caught in the act of pillaging and were administered a defeat at the hands of Greek mercenaries. To the chaplain of the count, Alexius now became the "perfidious Emperor."

Raymond d'Aguilers, who exhibits a capacity for missing important events in his master's life, was apparently not with Raymond in Constantinople, and his account reveals him again with lack of comprehension or interest in the problems which confronted the Provençal leader. Raymond arrived in the suburbs

of Constantinople April 21. He rested and awaited an audience
with the basileus on the following day. No eyewitness has left
us a description of this meeting, but we have a colorful account
from Albert of Aachen of crusading audiences with the emperor.
According to him, the princes of Gaul appeared in purple and
gold garments trimmed with ermine. Entering the presence of
Alexius, they knelt and received a kiss from him. We may assume
that Raymond was welcomed with the same pomp and circum-
stance, but his chaplain only states that his master was honorably
received at the Byzantine court. Anna informs us that her father
respected Raymond because of his wisdom, sincerity, purity of
life, and his truthfulness.

The conversations of the Count of Saint-Gilles and the emperor
lasted for four days, April 22–26, 1097. Their problems arose from
a number of sources. Apparently, Urban and Alexius had different interests at heart and consequently divergent hopes concerning the ultimate accomplishments of the *militia Christi*.
Alexius desired the return of the Byzantine themes to his empire;
Urban hoped to regain the Holy Sepulcher for Christendom. If
these two interests could be practically linked, the movement
would have a greater chance of success. At this juncture of the
expedition, Alexius was confronted by poorly controlled Latin
forces, which, according to past record, were more of a menace
to his kingdom than a probable source of aid. In this situation
he was seeking to make crusading leaders his vassals or his
mercenaries. It was in the midst of these new vassals of the
emperor that Raymond found himself when he arrived in Constantinople. Bohémond, former foe of Alexius, had become his
supporter in maneuvering for advantage in his service. Other
crusading leaders, who had done homage to Alexius and were
there at Constantinople, were perhaps dreaming of conquests
along the road to the Holy Sepulcher.

Raymond at the beginning of the conversations sought to
recall the figures in the negotiations to the high idealism of their
quest, if we can believe Raymond d'Aguilers, who couches the
matter in somewhat stylistic form. When Alexius demanded
homage and fidelity from the Count of Saint-Gilles after the
manner of the other leaders, Raymond replied that he knew

no other Master than the One for whom he had left his country. Nevertheless, he would place his army under the command of Alexius if he would lead it to Jerusalem. We may view this diplomatic maneuver perhaps as a feint in the game of shadow boxing in which Raymond and the basileus would engage in the next few days. The emperor temporized. He explained that Constantinople could not be left to the whims of the fierce tribes, the Germans, Hungarians, and the Kumans. Perhaps here the emperor sought to suggest the plight of his city, surrounded as it was by poorly disciplined Latins.

Into this impasse a lively element was introduced with the arrival of the news of the mistreatment of the count's army by imperial mercenaries. Hot words ensued. Raymond accused the emperor of ordering an attack upon his men. Alexius charged the Provençals with pillaging. Other crusading leaders, now vassals of Alexius, intervened to appease Raymond, who sought means to avenge the losses of his army. Duke Godfrey and Robert, Count of Flanders, reminded him that it was wrong for fellow Christians to quarrel. Bohémond threatened to join the cause of the emperor if Raymond failed to make peace. Perhaps at Raymond's demand, since this was his method of settling such disputes, the matter was put to trial, Bohémond placed in hostage for the emperor, and the cause considered. Raymond, whose peers in the matter were newly attached to the basileus, understandably lost in the litigation; however, with suitable treatment of the complaint accomplished, he turned again to his negotiations with Alexius. Perhaps this loss was of advantage to him, for Alexius showed himself anxious to appease the count by offering gifts. Obviously, the emperor would not wish an open break with Raymond, when the Provençal army was close at hand and angry from past humiliation.[8]

Raymond and Alexius must at this juncture have had one common desire uppermost in their minds, the Christian army's crossing of the Arm of Saint George and their subsequent march into Asia Minor. What part Adhémar played in their eventual concord is uncertain. No eyewitness states the exact date of the arrival of the Bishop of Le Puy in Constantinople. From the poor chronology of Raymond d'Aguilers, we infer that he arrived before the Count of Toulouse made an accord with the emperor, and that as a churchman he was excused from commitments to Alexius. The author of the *Gesta* infers that the bishop arrived after the convention of the two leaders. As a result the issue remains unsettled. Many modern historians, perhaps on the assumption that Adhémar would have sought to compromise the issue had he been there, have placed the bishop by Raymond's side exerting a mollifying influence. Yet the need for such influence is not apparent. The accord with Alexius does not reflect Raymond's deviation from his purpose as first announced —the furtherance of the army's journey to Jerusalem.

We may infer that the emperor was due, according to the count's thinking and Urban's planning, a pact or agreement asserting their mutual relations and security. When the emperor again asked for the count's homage, Raymond refused, "pro capitis periculo." As we have no evidence that there was in the situation cause for alarm for Raymond's person, we may resort to the wide connotation of the noun *caput* and think that here again he countered with legal terminology in defense of his position.

In the over-all picture presented by the chroniclers close to the events, we seem to see the count committing himself according to the custom of his land. Having more respect for legal contracts than symbolic acts and ever guarding his position as head of his army and of matters pertaining to his possessions, Raymond chose to ally himself with Alexius, and he agreed to respect the possessions of the emperor. If this oath followed the usual form for such alliances in southern France, as later references and actions of participants appear to confirm, then Raymond agreed to give no aid and counsel to those who menaced the emperor's possessions, and to return to Alexius, faithfully and without trickery, those possessions of the emperor which he himself might recover. By this means, the Count of Saint-Gilles, with the counsel of his companions, secured the progress and support of the crusade at this point of the journey without prejudicing his own position either by vassalage or by mercenary status.[9]

Alexius made commitments along with the agreements of the other crusading leaders. The general tenor of these pacts has

come to us through a combination of sources. Alexius promised
to furnish markets for provisions, to protect pilgrims, and to
pay crusaders for towns seized. He also promised to furnish
military aid, first under the leadership of Taticius and afterward possibly under his own direction. This assistance to the
crusade implied benefits expected or hoped for by the emperor
as the army advanced toward Jerusalem. The crusading leaders
demonstrated, at Nicaea and through their quarrels at Antioch,
their knowledge that they had sworn to return to the emperor
the themes which they freed from Moslem control. To justify
themselves in later breaking faith with the emperor and in their
opposition to Raymond's stand in defense of Alexius' rights,
other leaders would avoid the stigma of perjury by assuming the
position that the basileus had first broken faith, and in so doing
freed them from their oaths. To cloud the issue, we do not know
the boundaries Alexius had in mind for his possessions.[10]

As for the army, the little people, and the chroniclers, the
progress of affairs in Constantinople could only appear to them
through a fog of uncertainty and distress. Surrounded as their
journey was with the aura of mysticism, it was hard for them to
realize the necessity for Greek aid. In their poverty, they could
only resent the agreement neither to pillage the emperor's possessions nor to exact tribute along their march. Similar personal displeasure can be detected in the chaplain's complaint that Alexius
punished his stubborn master, the Count of Saint-Gilles, by
withholding large gifts.

So emotional was the reaction to the stress of the situation that
historians have drawn from comments of participants that the
Count of Toulouse remained upon poor terms with Alexius until
months later, saying that he was driven then to restore friendly
terms with the basileus only because he sought to deprive Bohémond of Antioch in an effort to secure the city for himself. As
a result, Raymond's spirited stand before the emperor, one
which probably extricated the crusade from its mired position at
this point, has brought him only criticism from those historians
who ignore the evidence of Anna Comnena here. It was she who
described Raymond shining as "the sun amidst the stars." She
also states that her father warned the count against the treachery

of Bohémond, a leader who, at this juncture of the crusade, fared better with the pens of the chroniclers than did the Count of Saint-Gilles.

We cannot doubt that Raymond was angry over the treatment of his men; however, we can feel that his anger was partly histrionic and certainly brief. William of Tyre, who no doubt follows Albert of Aachen, relates that the emperor accorded favorable treatment to the Provençal leader. Alexius, probably realizing that he could not make a mercenary out of Raymond, came to the conclusion that their objectives did not conflict, and carried out, at least for a time, the terms of their alliance. Raymond himself remained in or near Constantinople until May 10, 1097. In this decision the count, who had the largest contingent of men to cross the straits, must have been guided by considerations of supply and supervision. The movement of his army into Asia Minor had to be arranged for, as well as supplies and provisions for his men.[11]

Other crusading armies, smaller and more maneuverable, were already preparing to move toward Nicaea. The Provençals, slowed by their numbers in crossing to Asia Minor, would be among the last to approach Nicaea, and the Count of Saint-Gilles, lingering in the rear, would rejoin his troops before they reached the besieged city. Critics have often used Raymond's delay, April 26 to May 10, 1096, to infer that he sulked over his relations with the emperor. Anna, however, relates that her father took Raymond into his confidence, and that the other leaders awaited the arrival of Isangeles (Raymond) believing that the basileus would come with him. Albert writes of Raymond remaining in the city for fifteen days, during which time he received gifts from the emperor. William of Tyre also relates that Raymond tarried in Constantinople and was rewarded by Alexius with gifts.

Meanwhile, the march to Nicaea was uneventful. Contingents of the crusading armies left their encampment at Pelecanum under the leadership of Godfrey, Count Robert of Flanders, and Tancred, nephew of Bohémond. Accompanied by a force of Byzantine troops led by Manuel Butumites, they arrived before the walls of the city as early as May 6. However, the assembling of the army was slow and the formal besieging of the city was delayed until May 14. The lack of opposition en route to Nicaea portended the fate of the beleaguered city.

Nicaea was strongly fortified both by nature and by the towers of the Byzantines. Raymond d'Aguilers relates that on the west side a very long lake protected the city while upon three sides a ditch filled with water offered an obstacle to the crusaders. Particularly distressing to them was the line of impregnable fortifications with their crisscrossed loopholes that made an advance particularly hazardous. Kilij Arslan, Selchükid sultan, must likewise have thought highly of the defenses of Nicaea; or perhaps, remembering the fate of the Peasants' Crusade, he despised the strength of the new armies which confronted him. He had left his wife and children within the walls of Nicaea while he occupied himself elsewhere with fighting the Dānishmendid leaders.

In the early excitement of the investment of Nicaea, the Christians raced their horses in front of the defenders of the city, often approaching the towers in open defiance and with unfortunate results. Stark reminders of the fate of the peasants had heightened their fury, but the hardened Turks were not impressed by the bellicose display. The corpses of Christians dangling from the Turkish walls and the severed heads of Turks catapulted into Nicaea were grim reminders that the road to the Holy Sepulcher was a perilous one. But the leaders were aware of the siege problems and turned their attention to them. Godfrey and his men settled down to watch the northern wall while Tancred and later Bohémond camped to the east of the town, The southern gate was left for the Provençals, who were yet to arrive.

From within the town defenders dispatched messages to Kilij Arslan urging him to hasten to their aid and to use the southern entrance, as it was left unguarded. Crusaders were able to capture two Turkish scouts, one of whom survived to reveal news of reinforcements. Christian chieftains, alarmed over the unhappy news, rushed messengers to the Count of Saint-Gilles, who was now en route to Nicaea, begging him to hasten to their aid. The Provençals marched through the night and were before Nicaea at sunrise May 16 with banners flying and armor gleaming.

Ensuing events are confused. Western eyewitnesses leave the

impression that the relieving Turks were routed in one encounter. Apparently, Raymond had scarcely disposed of his baggage before a band of Turks descended upon him, only to be put to rout by Provençal forces. Followers of Godfrey also engaged the Selchükids in this encounter. Anna, who may be suspect in military matters, speaks of two attacks. According to her, Raymond, upon arrival before the city, put to rout one Turkish attack. On the following day the main forces of Kilij Arslan attacked the Provençals, who bore the brunt of the action, although the combined forces assisted. At the end of the day, after heavy losses by the crusaders, the Turks withdrew. Whoever may be correct, we may feel certain that by May 21 the siege was in full operation, and the garrison of Nicaea had been left to its fate by the sultan.

Provençals bore a large part of the siege operations, and in contrast to the uneasy days before Constantinople when the imperial mercenaries guarded and skirmished with the Provençals, there now was every appearance of unity among the Greeks and Latins. As a result, no doubt, of happy accord between Alexius and Raymond, the emperor's general Taticius, with two thousand peltasts, pitched camp in the sector near the Count of Saint-Gilles and aided siege operations materially. Alexius sent novel siege weapons to the crusaders, who were not properly equipped to besiege large cities, and the Westerners in turn kept the emperor informed of their fighting prowess by sending him sacks of Turkish heads. However, despite this unity and the belated arrival of Stephen of Blois and Robert, Count of Normandy, no progress was made toward the capture of Nicaea.

Anna relates that Raymond (still known to her as Isangeles) ordered the construction of a large circular tower, which upon completion was moved against the side of a tower named Gonates. Probably on June 10, under the protection of this tortoise and a cover from crossbows, Provençals dug under the Turkish fortification, replacing the stone foundation with logs. Their hope that the burning of the logs would topple Gonates proved in vain because the defenders worked throughout the night to repair the damage. In the meanwhile, the crusaders had solicited additional Greek aid, as they learned that the blockade was incomplete as long as Lake Ascanius was open to Turkish boats. In deference to this request, Alexius ordered boats to be hauled overland and launched on the lake. Using a type of psychological warfare from which the Count of Saint-Gilles may have drawn some lessons for his later dealings with the Turks, Butumites manned the boats with extra standards, created a great noise with trumpets and battle drums, and so frightened the inhabitants that, according to the chroniclers, they realized the futility of further resistance.

Alexius, thus close to his barbaric allies, who encouraged themselves by reminiscences of the bloody prowess of Maccabeus, must have shuddered at the thought of the sack of Nicaea by the Latins. As the city was to be returned to him, it would be his own domain that they ravaged; so again he sought to protect himself from this horde which Urban had called into being. He let the Latins discover their own weakness before the walls of the city. He then offered generous terms to the besieged Turks, and as a result on June 19 standards of the basileus flew from the towers of Nicaea, and the rank and file of crusaders knew that the Greeks possessed the town.[12]

Immediately misunderstanding arose because many of the crusaders had anticipated booty from pillaging. There seems little doubt, however, that the leaders of the army recognized that Alexius had acted in accord with their agreement. They appeared to recognize or to be cognizant of the terms of surrender, and to accept Alexius' disposals concerning the Latin army. Latins were forbidden to enter Nicaea except in small groups. Raymond d'Aguilers states that he promised the army gold, silver, and horses found in the town. He would, in addition, found a Latin monastery there and a refuge for the poor. Although Alexius was to abide by his promises, the lesser people, bitterly disappointed over the turn of affairs, complained of Greek treachery. The author of the *Gesta* felt that punishment was due the Turks and relates that many of the poor among the Latins died during the siege. Raymond d'Aguilers wrote that Alexius failed to carry out his pledge in such a manner that as long as he lived people would curse him and call him traitor. This stamp upon Emperor Alexius has lasted much longer than the count's chaplain could have anticipated. Years later Ordericus Vitalis wrote that jealousy of the crusaders prompted the Byzantine leader to accept the surrender of the Turkish garrison; and through the centuries Raymond's name has been subject to reproach for supporting the agreements with the Basileus.

That the violence of these attacks was born of pique of the moment rather than of over-all attitude toward the proceedings at this time, is demonstrated by the fact that the chroniclers often contradict themselves or reflect later attitudes created by Norman propaganda attacking the Greeks. The author of the *Gesta,* although he speaks of the poor starving, also writes that Alexius gave alms to them. Fulcher of Chartres tells us that the princes were richly rewarded and that the needy received copper coins. Stephen of Blois indicates that the hungry pilgrims received grain during the siege as a result of supplies sent by the Byzantines. Anselm of Ribemont in writing to Manasses, Archbishop of Rheims, indicates that there was good feeling between Latins and Greeks after the fall of Nicaea. However, the agreements with Alexius which would dominate affairs at Nicaea, would suffer the strain of increasing distance. In the upper ranks, individual aspirations in the months to come would undermine the accord; and in the lower ranks, the exploitation and extermination of Turks as enemies of God would overbear any consideration that these enemies of God should be preserved to pay tribute to the Greeks.[13]

Yet now, immediately after Nicaea and in furtherance of his pact with the Latin princes, Alexius summoned the leaders of the *militia Christi* to meet him at Pelecanum. The meeting was to serve the double purpose of rewarding the chieftains and securing oaths of loyalty from those who had escaped such commitments at Constantinople. In the course of the meeting on June 22, 1097, all leaders present, with the exception of Tancred, swore their allegiance without incident. This stubborn Norman nephew of Bohémond created a violent scene. He went so far as to insult Palaeologus, Byzantine noble and friend of Alexius, before he was induced to take the oath of homage to the emperor. The basileus then distributed gifts, thereby, we are told, pleasing some and disappointing others.

The Count of Saint-Gilles was absent from the meeting, and Chalandon has considered this absence sufficient grounds to maintain that Raymond's ill humor over small gifts caused him to remain at home. Stephen of Blois, an ardent admirer of the Byzantine wealth, writes that he also was absent from Pelecanum, and that the emperor was pleased by his attention to duty rather than his running after gifts at Pelecanum. It is reasonable to assume that Raymond's excuse for absence at Pelecanum is more valid than that of Stephen, for the count had already made his accord with the emperor. As he was neither a vassal nor a mercenary of the basileus, he need expect no reward at Pelecanum. In his long conversations at Constantinople, he had no doubt settled his affairs with Alexius, and, as had Stephen of Blois, already participated in the benefits of the Byzantine treasury.

The fall of Nicaea and the meeting at Pelecanum brought to a close the first phase of the journey to Jerusalem. Almost a year had elapsed from the time the Provençals had left their homes, yet they had experienced few reverses. Although they had learned to dislike their Christian brothers, the Greeks, they had in most cases experienced the bounty of these allies. They had traversed their lands and through their assistance had reached Asia Minor. Unequipped as they were for laying serious siege to large cities, the crusading army had, through the aid and connivance of the Greeks, reversed the Turkish contempt for the Latin rabble and brought Moslems to respect the forces of the Cross. In the next phase of their quest, the march through Anatolia and the capture of Antioch, they would suffer bitter fighting. Weakened by lack of Greek support and Norman-Provençal differences, the *militia Christi* would face the Moslems without the cunning of Alexius.[14]

NOTES

1. Willelmus Tyrensis, *Historia rerum in partibus transmarinis gestarum* in *RHC Occ.,* I, 97; Röhricht, *op. cit.,* p. 76; *The Alexiad,*

p. 254. Some have conjectured that Anna referred to Isoard of Mison, Viscount of Gap and Count of Die. For further information on William of Tyre, see A. C. Krey, "William of Tyre: The Making of an Historian in the Middle Ages," *Speculum,* XVI (1941); also the E. A. Babcock and A. C. Krey translation of William's work; a recent article on William is excellent, see Hans Eberhard Mayer, "Zum Tode Wilhelms von Tyrus," in *Archiv für Diplomatik* (1959–1960).

2. William of Tyre, *op. cit.,* p. 97.

3. Raymond d'Aguilers, *op. cit.,* pp. 235–36. Raymond's description carries liturgical reminiscences: "Sclavonia etenim est tellus deserta, et invia et montuosa" (Psalm 62:3, "In terra deserta, et invia, et inaquosa," Constantinus de Tischendorf, *Biblia sacra Latina,* p. 587); "per abrupta montium et condensa silvarum persequi" (Saint Ambrose, "Enarratio in Psalmum 1," c. 976, "praerupta montium, densa sylvarum"). This is evidence that Raymond d'Aguilers was intelligent, clever, and well schooled in church writing.

4. Steven Runciman, "The First Crusaders' Journey Across the Balkan Peninsula," in *Byzantion,* XIX (1949). All historians of the First Crusade are indebted to Hagenmeyer for his dating of events. However, some dating must remain conjectural. Comte Paul Riant, "Inventaire critique des lettres historiques des croisades," in *Archives de l'Orient latin,* I, 123; Raymond d'Aguilers, *op. cit.,* p. 236. See William M. Daly, "Christian Fraternity, the Crusaders, and the Security of Constantinople, 1097–1204; The Precarious Survival of an Ideal," in *Medieval Studies,* XXII (1960).

5. It is probable that Urban had an understanding that Alexius would furnish the Provençals a market upon their arrival in Greek territory. See Urban papa, *Epistolae et privilegia,* in *MPL,* CLI, 485; Raymond d'Aguilers, *op. cit.,* pp. 236–37; William of Tyre, *op. cit.,* I, 98–99, Anna, *op. cit.,* p. 249.

6. Raymond d'Aguilers, *op. cit.,* pp. 237–38.

7. *Gesta,* p. 30. We have used the Latin work of Louis Bréhier, *Histoire anonyme de la première croisade,* for the text of the *Gesta.*

8. *Gesta,* p. 32; Raymond d'Aguilers. *op. cit.,* p. 238.

9. We have discussed the stand of Raymond at length. See John Hugh Hill and Laurita L. Hill, "The Convention of Alexius Comnenus and Raymond of Saint-Gilles," in *AHR,* LVIII (January, 1953). Runciman continues to repeat in *The First Crusade* that Raymond took an oath of non-injury. He fails to point out that this oath as a convention protected property rights without involving vassalage. Rosell, *op. cit.,* I, 130–31; *Petri Exceptiones Legum Romanorum,* in Friedrich Carl von

Savigny, *Geschichte des Römischen Rechts im Mittelalter,* II, 325; Paul
Vinogradoff, *Roman Law in Medieval Europe,* pp. 32, 35; Dietrich
Shäfer, "Honor, citra, cis im Mittelalterlichen Latein," in *Sitzungs-
berichte der Preussischen Akademie der Wissenschaften,* p. 376.

10. R. B. Yewdale, *Bohémond I, Prince of Antioch,* p. 44; Fulcher,
op. cit., p. 332; Gislebertus, *Chronicon Hanoniense,* in *MGH SS.* XXI,
504; Ekkehardus, *Hierosolymita,* pp. 143–44; Robert the Monk, *op. cit.,*
p. 749.

11. Ferdinand Chalandon, "Essai sur le règne d'Alexis Ier Comnène
(1081–1118)," pp. 186–87; Grousset, *op. cit.,* p. 28; A. C. Krey, "A neglected Passage in the *Gesta,*" in *Munro Essays,* pp. 75–76; *The Alexiad,*
pp. 267–68; William of Tyre, *op. cit.,* pp. 104–105; Albert of Aachen,
op. cit., pp. 314, 317–18. Ordericus Vitalis has a story which duplicates
the story of Raymond's desire to attack the emperor, with the exception
that he uses Bohémond's name instead of that of the Count of Saint-
Gilles. Ordericus Vitalis, *Historia ecclesiastica libri tredecim,* in *MPL,*
CLXXXVIII, 663–64.

12. *Gesta,* pp. 36–38; *The Alexiad,* pp. 269–72; Raymond d'Aguilers,
op. cit., p. 239. See R. C. Smail, *Crusading Warfare (1097–1193). A Contribution to Medieval Military History* for an excellent account of the
military encounters of the crusaders.

13. Raymond d'Aguilers, *op. cit.,* p. 240; *Gesta,* p. 42; Ordericus
Vitalis, *op. cit.,* p. 667; Heinrich Hagenmeyer, *Die Kreuzzugsbriefe aus
den Jahren 1088–1100,* pp. 138, 144–45.

14. Chalandon, *op. cit.,* p. 167; James A. Brundage, "An Errant
Crusader: Stephen of Blois" in *Traditio,* 1960.

IV

THE CAPTURE OF ANTIOCH

PRESSED EVER by the clergy to regain the Holy Sepulcher, the Christian militia tarried but a short time in the environs of Nicaea. Breaking camp on June 26, 1097, various contingents resumed the journey during the following two or three days. Provençals departed on June 28 and rejoined the other armies by a bridge which spanned the Gallus river near Leucae. In the early morning of June 29 crusading forces divided, perhaps as Fulcher states, to secure supplies. In most instances government of the conduct of the armies was the result of decisions reached in councils of their leaders. Chroniclers, not understanding military problems or honest differences of opinion when they arose, frequently confuse us as to the policies of their leaders by attributing to them homiletic motives of venial or mortal sin. In this case Raymond d'Aguilers blames the rashness of Bohémond for separation of the armies on the march.

For whatever reason the division occurred, we know that troops under Bohémond, Tancred, Robert of Normandy, and Stephen of Blois veered to the right, while those of Godfrey of Bouillon, Hugh of Vermandois, Robert, Count of Flanders, and Raymond of Saint-Gilles took the left road, which lay to the northeast. On the evening of June 30, scouts of the first group discovered troops of the Sultan Kilij Arslan, who waited near Dorylaeum to attack the Christians. This advance information gave Bohémond an opportunity to display his military genius. Hastily the knights dismounted from their horses. Women and pilgrims, gathered within the circle of warriors, prepared to carry water to the fighters. Shortly thereafter Turkish cavalry charged the crusaders, who at this time were unaccustomed to an open type of warfare. Probably screaming "Allah Akbar!" ("God is great!") Turks wheeled, shot their arrows, and rode past the Christians, who were bewildered by their diabolical sounds and the speed of their Arab horses. In the meanwhile a messenger dispatched by Bohémond carried news of his plight to the other group of crusaders, who thereupon rushed with all haste to the relief of their embattled comrades. The Turks faltered upon sight of reinforcements, and their indecision was soon turned to rout by a flanking movement of Bishop Adhémar of Le Puy. In their success Raymond d'Aguilers reports supernatural protection similar to that which Judas Maccabeus had when two invulnerable horsemen led his hosts. Deserters from enemy forces related such intervention to the chaplain, and that cleric believed the report on the evidence of the many dead, masters and their horses, along the way.

This victory over the Moslem forces at Dorylaeum removed Kilij Arslan as a threat and opened the route south. After a short rest crusaders resumed their journey on July 3 or 4, 1097; and from this time until October 20 they were engaged in making the tedious march to Antioch. No source indicates the exact route followed between Dorylaeum and Iconium. The author of the *Gesta* relates that they crossed desolate country where the *militia Christi* encountered tortures of a midsummer sun. Battle steeds perished; sheep, goats, and dogs pulled the baggage; pilgrims attempted to find sustenance and moisture in cactus, aloes, and spiny vegetation of the desert. Bréhier believes that the journey led across the desert plateau of Lycaonia to the east of the Sultan Daghi. Runciman traces their route through Polybotus, Pisidian Antioch, across the bare passes of the Sultan Daghi, and to Philomelium, where they encountered the hardships of the desert wastes until they reached Iconium on August 15. As a reward, no doubt, for the crusaders' accumulating reputation of fierceness and fighting prowess, Turks had abandoned this town and its fertile valley, and so here the army of God found welcome respite.[1]

In the course of the journey from Dorylaeum to Iconium, Raymond of Saint-Gilles had fallen ill. We do not know the nature of his illness, nor are we certain of the exact date, although Hagenmeyer has chosen August 5 as a probable time. For lack of eyewitness reports on the nature of his malady, we may conjecture that the old count fell victim to the heat of the desert. Raymond d'Aguilers, in one of his hagiographical episodes, relates that an obscure knight came to the tent of the Provençal leader with an assuring message from Saint Gilles. Couched in words reminiscent of Isaiah's behest from the Lord concerning the Biblical Hezekiah, the knight's good tidings were to the effect that the saint had intervened on the count's behalf, and that God would spare him. Nevertheless, so serious was the malady of the Count of Toulouse that the bishop of Orange read the Office of the Dead as the Provençal leader lay gasping for breath. In the absence of medical skills, the count's rapid recovery, as related by his chaplain, was little short of miraculous. His illness delayed the march for a short time, and he was probably with his army when it left Iconium.

Refreshed by their stay in Iconium and supplied with water, the crusaders marched to Heraclea, where they routed a Turkish force, perhaps on September 10. A few days later Tancred and Baldwin, the brother of Duke Godfrey, led a small detachment of Normans and Lotharingians into Cilicia. The successful exploits of Tancred in this area and his quarrel with Baldwin at Mamistra are of interest to the follower of the main crusading armies only inasmuch as they reveal the suggestion of a rift in the papal plan of the expedition and foreshadow a collapse of the hard-won Greek-Latin rapprochement of Constantinople, Nicaea, and Pelecanum. Some scholars seek to establish the fact that the expedition was sent into Cilicia for the strategic military purpose of securing aid from the inhabitants. Contemporary apologists for the later desertion of the crusade by Baldwin and Bohémond and their consequent absence from the fall of Jerusalem, declare that some lords had to remain behind to hold secure the conquered lands. However, this foray of Baldwin and Tancred, degenerating as it did into a struggle between land-hungry nobles, is suggestive of interest in securing a foothold in the Levant rather than desire to procure supplies for the march to Jerusalem.

The main force of crusaders continued under Raymond of Saint-Gilles, Bohémond, and Godfrey, moving from Heraclea to Caesarea after an uneventful ten days. The army then marched hurriedly to Placentia, where a besieging Turkish force fled before the crusaders could overtake them. Again the growing reputation of the soldiers of the Cross had apparently aided them. Peter of Aulps, a Provençal knight in the service of Alexius, accepted command of the town, and the army continued its march from Placentia to Coxon, where the crusaders recuperated from October 5 to 9 in this well provisioned Armenian town.[2]

Now came news that the Turks had abandoned Antioch. Acting upon the rumor, Raymond called a council of his Provençals, and upon their decision he sent a vanguard to verify the report. Peter of Castillon, William of Montpellier, Peter of Roaix, and Peter Raymond of Hautpoul with five hundred knights rushed to carry out the command of the council. Arriving at a stronghold of Paulician heretics, they learned that the Turks were making preparations to defend Antioch. Unsuccessful then in this mission, Peter of Roaix and his followers separated from the others and entered the valley of Rugia. There they defeated the Turks and took possession of the town of Rusa after an enthusiastic reception from the Armenian inhabitants.

Yewdale, Bréhier, and others suggest that the Count of Toulouse had ambitions to seize Antioch at this early stage of the crusade. Their interpretation is drawn from the single statement of the *Gesta,* in which the author relates that Raymond decided in his council (*in suo invenit consilio*) to dispatch knights to Antioch. Yet we cannot gauge Raymond's actions here in failing to call a general council. In the face of ever decreasing threats from the Turks along the route, the contingents apparently scattered as they marched toward Antioch. Seemingly, Bohémond was not with the army, and Tancred and Baldwin had not returned from their venture in Cilicia. Haste was indicated and the Provençal knights were at hand.

It is possible that the leaders were not so sanguine as to believe that Turkish forces would give up Antioch as easily as a village, and that this light maneuverable force was merely a scouting party with a companion objective of securing a base of supply in advance of the cumbersome, slow moving pilgrim force. Raymond's followers had suffered all along the route because their slowness placed them in the rear. As they drew farther from Constantinople, it would be more difficult to supply them except from the land that they traversed. In this situation even the foot soldiers learned to slip out of camp during the night, so that they might secure supplies in the new territory. Eyewitness reports do not condemn Raymond's procedure, and we do not find in them basis for the supposition that relations between Raymond and Bohémond were strained as a result.[3]

The main army now followed the vanguard closely from Coxon across the Anti-Taurus, which chroniclers described as the diabolical mountains. Horses and riders plunged from its narrow paths into the canyons below. Mounted knights sold or threw away their heavy armor. Then, on October 13, the crusaders came to Marash, where they received a warm welcome from the Armenian population. The hardships of the past were momentarily forgotten in the midst of plenty. Here they were rejoined by Bohémond, who had been away pursuing Dānishmendids, and by Baldwin, who had been in Cilicia. After a short rest, forces again divided with Baldwin abandoning the main army to make a foray which resulted in the establishment of the county of Edessa, the first of the important crusading states in the Levant.

The army moved toward Antioch, while a small detachment under Count Robert of Flanders attacked and captured the town of Artāh with the aid of the Armenian inhabitants. We have no eyewitness account of this action, but Albert of Aachen, whose testimony is taken by William of Tyre, informs us that a counterattack of a Turkish relief force failed to expel the Christians, thereby leaving the road to Antioch to the crusaders. Bernard, chaplain of the bishop of Le Puy, was made bishop of the town, a selection which would seem to furnish precedent for Raymond's similar action later in the crusade at Albara.

As the march continued, Christian forces moved into the valley of the Orontes. They converged upon the Iron Bridge, gateway from Marash and Aleppo. The *Gesta* mentions an encounter here. Albert tells us that Robert of Normandy had preceded the army so that he could detect any Turkish ambush. Approaching the Iron Bridge, the army saw an ancient structure built with marvelous skill and protected by two imposing towers. Turks launched a hail of arrows which felled horses and wounded knights. Despite these losses, crusaders, fired with enthusiasm by Adhémar, advanced upon the defenders and completely routed them. Concerning this skirmish, the *Gesta* informs us that Christians seized an enormous amount of booty—camels, mules, and asses, loaded with grain and wine.

In such manner we are told that crusaders rode high upon the wheel of fortune as they first caught sight of Antioch. Bohémond led the advance detachment as the army left the Iron Bridge behind and marched toward the city. Albert describes the scene. Soldiers of the Cross struck terror into the hearts of the defenders of the city. Christian shields were resplendent—golden, green, red, and multi-colored. Banners of gold and purple streamed among the knights. Helmets gleamed and armor shone as noble warriors sat their splendid war horses. However, this colorful picture from Albert's pen must be sobered by first-hand reports, which do not encourage the fanciful optimism of his narrative. Months of war, weather, and toil had left many a fine knight buried between Constantinople and Antioch. Many a banner was tattered, and nerves were frayed. Before the army were impressive rows of towers; and their dread implication to those who dared to attack Antioch led Raymond d'Aguilers to state that the city need fear neither the efforts of machines nor the assaults of men. An ominous silence gave crusaders little comfort. So it was in an atmosphere of foreboding that the Christians reached Antioch between October 20 and 22.[4]

Despite its apparent impregnability, the sight of the city called forth an ovation from those upon the scene. Antioch was sacred to Christian memory, and disaster was not new to it. Founded by Seleucus I of Syria in 300 B.C., it had withstood earthquakes as well as the horrors of siege and conquest at the hands of Persians and Arabs. It was refortified by Byzantine engineers only to be lost to the Turks. The Orontes River, Mount Silpius, and surrounding marshy land gave natural barriers. These natural defenses had been supplemented by three to four hundred towers strategically placed to ward off any attack. Five important gates gave the city access to the outside world. The Gate of Saint Paul lay to the east and guarded the road to Aleppo. Following the walls of the city as they meandered to the north and west and then turned southward, we can locate the smaller gates, the Gate of the Dog and the Porta Ducis, so named for Godfrey's investment of it. After these two gates the Bridge Gate opened to those who journeyed from the sea or the coastal road from Asia Minor. Then came the Gate of Saint George, which admitted visitors from Latakia. There was a minor gate beyond as the walls turned northeast to complete their circuit through Mount Silpius to the road to Aleppo and the Gate of Saint Paul. It was the Iron Gate, which guarded a gorge cut through the mountain. The city itself within these spacious walls had room to house and feed an army that could resist a long siege.

Strong as it was, however, Antioch had its weakness—treachery from a polyglot population. This flaw in its armor was magnified by the timidity of the Turkish garrison, while Yaghi Siyan, its defender, depended upon intrigue to hold his enfeebled state. By playing his two rivals, Dukak of Damascus and Kerbogha of Mosul, against his overlord Ridvan, he had alienated his possible allies. Alarmed by successes of crusaders, he suppressed or drove out many Christians whom he had tolerated. At the same time he dispatched his son, Shams-ad-Daulah, and other envoys to beg aid from his rivals. Overlooking the Machiavellian predilections of Yaghi Siyan, Dukak and Kerbogha offered their services, as did Tughtigin of Damascus and Janāh-ad-Daulah, who was atabeg of Homs. The shortsighted Ridvan, however, did not come to his aid immediately.

While Yaghi Siyan remained peacefully within the walls of Antioch and hoped for hurried reinforcements, crusading leaders temporized. One group suggested that they await the coming of Alexius before undertaking the destruction of the Turkish garrison. Taticius, no doubt aware of the difficulties of a siege, probably advised leaders to seize near-by castles and towns and await developments. The other group, under the leadership of Raymond of Saint-Gilles, wished to start operations against the Turks immediately. Runciman assumes that Raymond wished to assault the walls. On this issue, however, the count's chaplain only confuses us by giving a short peroration of his master, the goodness of God, and trust in His mercy. Thus we cannot be sure that the count urged more than an opening siege of Antioch on the arrival of the armies. That the crusaders might have stormed the city successfully on their arrival is even more doubtful.[5]

As the crusading chiefs considered the siege of the city, it became immediately apparent that the nature of the fortifications and the natural barriers dictated an attack from the north and east. Bohémond and his Normans anchored the eastern line as they watched the Gate of Saint Paul. Raymond and Adhémar, along with the Provençal troops and knights, guarded the Gate of the Dog, often referred to as Warfaru. Godfrey and his Lotharingians pitched their tents near the Duke's Gate. The Bridge Gate and the Gate of Saint George were at first left unguarded. Here, then, for fifteen days crusaders enjoyed the plenty of the land with little concern for the infrequent watchmen who showed themselves from the towers of Antioch; and Yaghi Siyan, behind his high walls, depended upon Armenian spies to keep him informed of movements of his enemies.

During this time the position of the Provençals is but poorly described by eyewitnesses; and only through Albert of Aachen and William of Tyre can we find a partly satisfactory account of their participation in early siege operations. Raymond's men had pitched their camp close to the river and near a bridge which spanned some marshy land leading to the Gate of the Dog. While Turks watched their movements, perhaps on October 24, Provençals and doubtless Lotharingians constructed a bridge of boats, probably pontoons, which enabled foraging parties to return rapidly to the south bank of the Orontes whenever they were attacked by Turks riding from the Bridge Gate. Provençals, like other crusaders, occupied neighboring cities to forage for themselves and to cut off supplies to Antioch. Ralph of Caen states that Raymond's men occupied Rubée, Rhosus, Arcican, and Belmesyn. We may assume that the Provençals made their headquarters in the area of Chastel-Rouge and Arzghān when they were not pressing the attack on Antioch.[6]

An early lull in hostilities led many knights to take quarters in distant castles. Soldiers of the Cross wasted food without thought of approaching famine. Spies reported this situation to Yaghi Siyan, and Turks began their attacks on November 4. Moslem raids were particularly costly to the men and horses in Raymond's camp. These thrifty Provençals, perhaps happiest when they were foraging and pilfering, now found their food supply diminished and their ranks thinned.

As these difficulties continued, the Turkish garrison of Hārim on the road to Aleppo attacked from the rear and jeopardized Norman forces. Bohémond met this threat by tricking the defenders of Hārim into open fight and destroying them. Neither the *Gesta* nor Raymond d'Aguilers tells us of Provençal retaliation against guerrilla tactics of the enemy; however, Albert goes into lengthy detail. He relates that they first attempted to take hammers and demolish the stone bridge leading from the Dog's Gate. Its solid masonry, however, defied their best efforts. A hastily built tower served for a time to check enemy raids from the gate; however, incited by the death of an illustrious warrior, Turks surged across the bridge and burned the structure. Christians then attempted to batter the gate with three mangonels, but this availed them little. Finally, hundreds of them pushed stones and giant timbers across the gate, and so ended the harrying of their camp.

During this time, perhaps November 17, Genoese vessels arrived in Saint Simeon, the port of Antioch, apparently in co-operation with the land forces in what seems to have been a prearranged plan. Joy in their initial successes and welcome news of the Genoese did not solve the more pressing problems of the hit-and-run tactics of the Turks. A council of leaders assembled and agreed to build and fortify a tower on a hill which guarded the approach to Bohémond's camp. Members of the council promised to take turns in guarding the tower, which they named Maregart.

Affairs in the crusading camp proceeded in such fashion until December, when ill fortune began to plague the Christians anew. Food supplies dwindled, morale became low, Godfrey fell ill, and Count Robert of Normandy left the army to enjoy the comforts of peace in Latakia. To meet this situation another council of leaders was called, and after some debate Bohémond and

Robert, Count of Flanders, were chosen to lead a foraging expedition up the Orontes valley. To Raymond and Adhémar fell
the task of guarding the rear by watching over the enemy within
Antioch.

Following the departure of the foraging force, the well informed Yaghi Siyan attacked the besiegers on December 29.
Launching his attack from the Bridge Gate of the Turks, the
governor of Antioch sent forth his troops on what appeared to
be a customary maneuver. One version of the *Gesta* has led to
the belief that the assault was a sneak raid made by night (*nocte*).
The other version states that the attack was made cautiously
(*caute*). From the account of Raymond d'Aguilers, we may conclude that the fighting took place by daylight. It has further
been suggested that the count's men had occupied the higher
ground north of the Orontes near the bridge of boats, as the site
of their first camp was marshy. The chaplain of the count, however, leads us to believe that a detachment of Provençals crossed
to the north to meet the raiding Turks. Raymond, in any case,
quickly rallied his men, brought order to the footmen, and then
turned against the Turks with his mounted knights. Two Turks
were captured and killed in a manner reminiscent of the count's
treatment of the captive Slavs.

At this point plans of the princes regarding the safety of the
camp had every reason to succeed. The Provençal counterattack
had forced the enemy back on their bridge. But the fortunes of
war turned suddenly. Unruly foot soldiers deserted their places
and their standards to make an ill advised attack on fleeing Turks.
Some knights turned to pursue a riderless horse, and in so doing
led a general retreat. This retreat, impeded by the now massive
mob of footmen, rapidly became a rout. Victory turned into
panic. Defeated Turks rushed forth again to slaughter Christians.
Knights unhorsed by the disorderly rabble jumped into the river,
where they became victims of stones and arrows. The flight was
checked at the bridge of boats only after heavy losses. Adhémar
lost his standard bearer, and the Turks captured his standard of
the Blessed Mary. Planting this ensign on their wall, point down-
ward as a sign of their contempt, Moslems caused the Christians
great sorrow that the standard of the Virgin should be so defiled.

They sorrowed also for Bernard Raymond, a noble Provençal youth from Béziers, who lost his life along with some fifteen knights and twenty foot soldiers. We cannot be sure that Raymond lost the opportunity to force the Gate of the Bridge, but their recorded losses were such that despair prevailed in the camp.

Meanwhile, the foraging expedition, a motley group including some Provençals, marched under the leadership of Bohémond and Count Robert of Flanders. As the detachment searched unsuccessfully for supplies, a Turkish relief force under Dukak of Damascus attacked one wing of the troops under the count of Flanders and fled only after a brilliant maneuver by Bohémond. The chaplain of the count is reminded of battles of the Maccabees in the miraculous victory over such superior numbers of Turks; however, despite the valor of the foraging expedition, it did not accomplish its mission and returned to the camp at Antioch empty-handed.[7]

God now frowned upon the crusaders, at least so thought the chroniclers, who attributed His displeasure to the sins of adultery and avarice in the camp of the Christians. The Count of Saint-Gilles became ill. Northern lights appeared in the sky to warn the sinful of the wrath of God. Rains fell and cold chilled those who had thought the climate better than the climate of their homeland. Food was scarce and profiteers took advantage of the situation to drive hard bargains. Men deserted and horses died. Adhémar set aside three days beginning January 2, 1098, for fasting, almsgiving, and prayer. In this Jeremiah-like atmosphere, Raymond arose from his sickbed to call a council of the princes and the bishop of Le Puy. He announced that he would give five hundred marks of silver to the brotherhood. A knight who lost his horse was to be reimbursed from this silver or from other resources of the group. This policy, the chaplain tells us, enabled and even encouraged foraging, as those who lost weak and starving horses might expect to receive better ones in their places.

Despite this relief from the Count of Saint-Gilles and the brotherhood, crusaders had little cause for joy in the opening weeks of the year 1098. The chaplain informs us that they held a council in which they pledged themselves to continue the siege for seven years if necessary, and that all the chiefs with the ex-

ception of Raymond promised Bohémond possession of Antioch.
He has previously told us that Bohémond had threatened to leave
the siege as a ruse to support his aspirations concerning the city.
To add to the woes of the Christians, Taticius, commander of
the Byzantine contingent, departed from the army in the early
part of February, as a relief force under the now active Ridvan
of Aleppo approached Antioch. To meet the threat of this new
danger, crusading chieftains met in council in the tent of the
bishop of Le Puy. The result of this planning was the routing
of the forces of Ridvan on February 9 by a surprise attack, which
gave the Christians a choice of battle terrain.

The *Gesta,* in recounting these events, gives credit to Bohémond for both the planning and the execution of the maneuver.
His speech in council, the activity of his scouts, the inspiration
of his battle address, and the example of his constable are faithfully reported, along with the information that it was this same
Constable Robert, son of Girard, who, carrying the banner of
Bohémond, pressed the Turks even as a hungry lion rushes from
his lair and, thirsting for blood, comes among sheep and tears
them to pieces as they mill about. Other warriors, heartened by
this example, rallied to defeat the enemy. Raymond d'Aguilers
gives credit for the victory to the joint council of the princes
who devised the battle plan. The knights had the aid of God
and the advantage of surprise, since their cavalry slipped out of
camp in darkness to make their dawn attack. The chaplain describes the terrain, which so favored the victory, and adds the
information that they charged when they had driven the first line
of Turks back upon the second and confusion favored the Christians.

Hārim fell again to the crusaders as a result of Ridvan's defeat,
and the eastern approach to Antioch was sealed. Back in camp,
forces of Yaghi Siyan had discovered the helpless condition of
the footmen, although the knights had slipped quietly out of
camp the night before. Footmen, awaiting results of the cavalry
expedition, found Turkish forces from the city attempting to
break out from the gates of Antioch. Christian soldiers gave a
good account of themselves, but after a day's encounter, they welcomed the return of the heavily armed warriors, who sent the

besieged rushing back into Antioch, where from their walls they might view heads of their countrymen hanging from stakes and understand, according to the chaplain, God's displeasure for their defilement of the banner of the Blessed Virgin.[8]

On hand to view the results of this twofold victory were emissaries of al-Afdal, vizir of Egypt. Remaining for several weeks, this delegation sought an alliance with the Christians. Abhorring the Selchükids, whom they wished to eject from the Holy City, the Fātimids were willing to undertake a policy of duplicity by which the Westerners would hold Syria while they themselves took possession of Palestine. Christian leaders, adopting Eastern diplomacy, heaped gifts upon the embassy, showed them heads of decapitated Turks, and sent delegates with them on their return to Egypt. These negotiations, however, bore little fruit. The crusaders sought to deliver the Holy City. They could not compromise when their quest was at stake.

Reverses of Yaghi Siyan only increased sneak attacks by the Turks, who attempted to check the delivery of supplies from the port of Saint Simeon. To prevent these inroads, Raymond proposed that if the brotherhood would help him erect a tower, he would stand guard over it. Timely arrival on March 4 of a fleet, probably commanded by Edgar Atheling sailing under Alexius, offered hope for the new project. Bohémond and Raymond were chosen by the leaders to head a detachment to the port to secure supplies and workmen for the project. On the return trip, March 6, their contingents were ambushed by chattering and shouting Turks from the garrison. Christians were forced to abandon their supplies and flee precipitately.

Back in camp, troops bore the onslaught of Moslem warriors in an attack inspired by Turkish knowledge of the departure of the knights for Saint Simeon. A force of Christians, retaliating without attention to order and plan, were put to flight. Of the subsequent battle, which was fought as a result of the army's rally in camp, we have divergent accounts. The author of the *Gesta* gives Bohémond, who had detached himself from the battle on the port road and returned quickly to camp, credit for rallying the forces there by arousing them with news of the defeat. The chaplain writes that those in camp knew nothing of the defeat on the road to Saint Simeon. He cites Duke Godfrey and Ysoard of Ganges, a noble Provençal, as responsible for inspiring the victory. Albert seeks to give Godfrey his due without robbing Bohémond. The leaders of the defeated forces, according to his account, arrived after Godfrey had heard the news of defeat from a messenger and had roused the camp. Accounts converge at this point. Yaghi Siyan, encouraged and hoping for a great victory, sent forth his knights, commanded them to overcome or perish, and closed the gates behind them. The routed forces of Bohémond and Raymond were not only saved by the able rally of the army in camp, but Turks were slaughtered outside the Bridge Gate as they attempted to gain protection by returning to the city. To prevent more slaughter, Yaghi Siyan opened the gates to his defeated army.

Christian women of the city peered from the walls of Antioch as they secretly applauded the soldiers of Christ, who hacked and slew Turks to the number of fifteen hundred. Under cover of early morning darkness, distraught defenders buried their dead in the Moslem cemetery without the gates. Christians, particularly the poor, added to the spoils of the battle by exhuming bodies, robbing them of their gold, and cutting off their heads to the sorrow of the besieged.

With joy over the success of the battle and easing of their situation, all set themselves to the task of building the castle opposite the Bridge Gate. Construction was hastened by workmen from the port of Saint Simeon. Unconvinced of the victory of the crusaders until they saw the Turkish dead floating down the river, they then ventured to join the army and contribute their skill to the building of the fortification. Using stones from the Moslem cemetery, workers completed the new castle, La Mahomerie, within two weeks, perhaps by March 20.

The Count of Saint-Gilles took charge of this new fortification despite the objections of his men. Gaston de Béarn, Peter of Castillon, Raymond of Turenne, William of Montpellier, Gouffier of Lastours, and William of Sabran aided him in the task of holding the Turks in check. In this action chance dictated the emergence of the Count of Toulouse into the forefront of army enthusiasm. According to his chaplain, unsupported by other leaders, he displayed remarkable valor in a surprise skirmish with a large force of Turks. Noise of the encounter brought relief from the camp of the army, and La Mahomerie's value was proven. Sallies of the besieged from the Bridge Gate were now cut off, and Christians could call Raymond father and savior of the army.[9]

Only one main exit gate now remained unblocked. Through the Gate of Saint George the Moslems continued to pasture their horses and receive supplies. In this situation a council of crusaders, perhaps on April 5, decided to fortify a castle where the old monastery of Saint George stood. Tancred offered to accept command of this post if he were sufficiently paid. Apparently, the brotherhood agreed to pay him four hundred marks of silver, of which amount the Count of Saint-Gilles contributed one-fourth. Thus, by April, crusading hopes mounted as the blockade of the five great gates of Antioch—Gate of Saint Paul, Gate of the Dog, Gate of the Duke, Gate of the Bridge, and Gate of Saint George —shattered the hopes of defenders in the city. Tancred, at his new post, captured goods intended for the city; horses and mules pasturing outside the city were seized, and traders, now faced with a limited market, began to deal more leniently with Latins.

In the midst of these successes of the army, however, there were new dangers to come. Kerbogha, atabeg of Mosul, was massing his forces against the day when he would meet the Christian forces before Antioch. Crusaders, to counter this new threat, sought unsuccessfully to secure the neutrality of Dukak and to hasten the march of Alexius, who now had an army on the way to Antioch. Kerbogha meanwhile augmented his following by reinforcements from Bagdad, Persia, and Northern Mesopotamia. Approaching Antioch in a leisurely fashion, he wasted some three weeks in an abortive attempt to wrest Edessa from Baldwin. Yaghi Siyan played for time and, perhaps on May 15, through a treacherous ruse of offering to discuss surrender terms, massacred a small group of Christians, among whom was Galon, constable of the king of France.

In this troubled time of rumors, fears, and mounting tension brought on by the nearness of Kerbogha, the fate of Antioch was in the balance. Many crusaders fled the camp, best known of whom was Stephen of Blois, who took the road to Alexandretta with his knights, saying that his health no longer permitted him to remain at the siege. What happened in the camps of those who remained outside the walls of Antioch is an open question, as those who wrote of the betrayal and fall of Antioch have left us conflicting reports. Raymond d'Aguilers and some of the crusading letters lead us to believe that the city was delivered through treachery to the leaders of the army. The *Gesta* leaves us a detailed account of the city's deliverance to Bohémond and his outstanding service in the event.

If we follow the *Gesta,* which has unfortunately shown itself suspect in regard to Bohémond's rights to the city, and the *Gesta*'s continuators, we believe that for some time the Norman adventurer had been in communication with a renegade Armenian named Fīrūz, who had been converted to Mohammedanism. This man had several grievances. He had experienced an unfortunate business transaction, and his wife had been discovered in an affair with a man of the garrison. Disgruntled as a result, the traitor promised to betray his watch towers to Bohémond. Probably on May 25, Bohémond approached the council of princes and asked possession of Antioch for the leader who could win it. This offer was refused on the grounds that all who had suffered in the siege should share in the reward. A short time later, on May 29, Bohémond was granted an accord which promised him Antioch if he could bring about its fall, provided that the emperor failed to come and carry out his promises to the princes. Raymond d'Aguilers maintains, however, that the Count of Saint-Gilles never agreed to give the city to Bohémond.[10]

Presented with these conflicting statements and subsequent events, continuators and critics have chosen their own ingredients for historical accounts with the result that the Greek-Latin relations from April 1097 at Constantinople to the present time have been clouded by emotionalism and misconceptions. Alternately, Bohémond or the Count of Saint-Gilles is blamed for events to follow. Evidence for their motives is sought along the course of the crusade. Chalandon sees, in the chaplain's account of the opening week of 1098, evidence of Bohémond's plans to seize Antioch. Yewdale, in Bohémond's defense, urged that Raymond

d'Aguilers was confused in his chronology when he placed Bohémond's request for the city at so early a date.

The flight of Taticius has been another springboard for conjecture on Greek-Latin relations. Occasion of much indignation
in the crusading camp, the Byzantine leader is charged by the
author of the *Gesta* with abandoning the siege for fear he would
fall into the hands of the enemy. Raymond d'Aguilers states
that the Greek, whose name he almost forgot to mention because
it should be committed to oblivion, secretly fled, leaving his army
and granting to Bohémond Mamistra, Tarsus, and Adana. Anna,
however, believed that Bohémond frightened Taticius by telling
him that crusaders planned to take revenge upon him for their
misfortune. Some scholars have sought to use his flight to sub-
stantiate the idea that Bohémond broke off friendly relations
with the emperor at that time, and that Raymond of Saint-Gilles
then forgot his enmity toward Alexius in order to oppose Bohémond's aspirations for Antioch.

Of course, Raymond's enmity toward the emperor is pure conjecture, and Bohémond's friendship with him is suspect. In cor-
roboration of this, Anna states that her father was anxious to
get the Norman adventurer into Asia as quickly as possible so
that he could not corrupt the other leaders. She emphasized the
fact that Bohémond had few men and little money, and that her
father, who could "out-Cretan a Cretan," sought in his subsequent dealings to trick Bohémond with gifts and promises of high
office. Her father, she states, also warned the Count of Saint-Gilles
against the Norman's treachery. Anna's appraisal of the situation is borne out in part by Albert, who believed that Bohémond
coveted the lands of the emperor before the crusade and exon-
erated Godfrey from conniving with him.

Recent scholarship has also questioned Bohémond's friendship
with the emperor. It has been demonstrated that Alexius did not
promise Bohémond the area around Antioch. This purported
promise has been shown to be an interpolation in the *Gesta* made
later, when Bohémond had returned to the West to enlist aid
against the emperor. At this time he resorted to many tricks to
damage the reputation of his former ally, Alexius, and to justify

his own illegal seizure of Antioch. The wily Norman brought Scythians to Rome to show Pope Paschal that the basileus had allied himself with these barbarians. Eventually, his chicanery secured papal justification for his later war on the Byzantines in 1107.

In Bohémond's progression from hope to fruition concerning the possession of Antioch, we find it impossible to say when he chose to begin urging the princes openly in council to forsake their oaths and remain in perjury to the emperor. Common peril must have united the crusaders before Antioch and, however much he was personally responsible for the intrigue and the actual fall of the city, Bohémond must have recognized that he needed the cooperation of the army to succeed. The *Gesta's* reported accord of May 29 (granting Bohémond the city if he could win it and if Alexius did not come to fulfil his promises) does not reflect the proceedings of a council that thought Alexius was coming to its aid. Even after they were themselves besieged in Antioch, crusaders had not lost hope of the emperor's coming, and upon their routing of the besieging Turks, they sent an embassy inviting Alexius to come and receive the city. In the light of these events, the earlier statement of the chaplain concerning this promise seems to be a commentary upon a later argument. Furthermore, the *Gesta's* accord of May 29, couched in legal phraseology though it may be, seems to reflect opportunism born of subsequent events and arguments of the princes after the fall of the city and the defeat of Kerbogha.

Stirring of anti-Greek feeling, on the other hand, was ever an easy matter, and Bohémond may have played an early part in flogging this popular whipping boy for the failures of the army. Dissatisfied at Nicaea, the lesser people, who seemed to find their voice along with the petty clergy in the outpourings of the count's chaplain, were unhappy with the Greek alliance which brought them so little in worldly goods and kept the princes preoccupied with conquests of territory rather than with completion of the crusading objective. In such an atmosphere Bohémond alone shone for his activity, and the popularity of the count suffered because he urged the necessity of the Greek alliance. The departure of Taticius was noised far beyond its importance, and such reports as the chaplain's of his grants to Bohémond demonstrate the conflicting rumors which spread as his departure became known. He also tells us at this time of the unpopularity of the Count of Saint-Gilles, who was regarded as of little consequence, not that he had not done much, but because they all thought that he could do more. In this connection the cleric cites Raymond on two counts of deadly sin, sloth and avarice; however, as deadly sin was a clergyman's stock in trade, we can regard his use of it as technical rather than descriptive.[11]

Whatever may be the truth of the relations of Bohémond and Raymond before the fall of Antioch, we know that the secrecy with which the plan for its capture was handled added to the confusion of the eyewitnesses. Most of them, however, connect Bohémond with the proceedings. On June 2, 1098, according to the *Gesta*, he informed Godfrey of Bouillon, Robert of Flanders, Raymond of Toulouse, and Adhémar of Le Puy of his arrangements with Fīrūz and of the plan of attack on the city. It appears that Raymond entered wholeheartedly into the scheme and aided the Norman in his design. The attack was well planned. The garrison was lulled into a sense of security by secret maneuvers of the Latins. Under the cover of darkness, crusaders commanded by Bohémond marched to the Gate of Saint George near which was located one of the towers which Fīrūz had promised to deliver, the Tower of the Two Sisters. Faithful to his promise, the traitor permitted a small force to gain access to his stronghold. What followed is an often retold story. After reverses caused by a broken ladder, attackers from outside gained entrance by a postern gate and joined forces with those who scaled the walls. The Gate of Saint George and the Gate of the Bridge were flung open to bloodthirsty Christians, who hacked and slew men and women of the infidels (and perchance some of their own faith) in the city. Screams of the wounded and dying kept attackers well informed of the success of the carnage. Apparently the Provençals by the Bridge Gate were among the last to enter, because Raymond d'Aguilers wrote of the wailing of women and children within the city being heard in the count's castle. As dawn broke, Latins saw the banner of Bohémond waving from the highest spot in Antioch.

Throughout the day Westerners enjoyed sacking and looting the city. In the early stages of the fighting, Yaghi Siyan foolishly attempted to flee by way of a postern gate which led to the area guarded by Tancred. Wearied by flight, the Turkish chieftain was recognized, killed, and decapitated by native Armenians and Syrians. His bloody head brought pleasure to the soldiers of Christ, who saw the ineffable will of God which brought this tyrant to his just punishment. In this general massacre Raymond d'Aguilers took vicarious pleasure. Particularly pleasing to him was the sight of Turkish horsemen dashed to death as they plunged from a rocky precipice. Equally saddening to him was the thought of thirty horses with broken necks. Stench of the dead and rumor of the approach of Kerbogha, however, gave the Christians little time for joy. Their plans had fallen short of their goal. Lacking the citadel, now commanded by Yaghi Siyan's son, Shams-ad-Daulah, the army would be imprisoned in its own success.

As a result of this perilous situation and of internal dissension after the menace was removed, the crusade would many times in the days and months to come be on the verge of collapse. No satisfactory apportionment of the blame for these developments has been made, because we cannot fathom the interplay of personal aggrandizement, superstition, prejudice, and sincere religious feeling as it is presented to us by the pens of the eyewitnesses and their followers. Interest in securing personal footholds in the Levant was perhaps evident as early as the expedition of Tancred and Baldwin in Cilicia. Deterioration of the Greek-Latin rapprochement could be seen as the armies drew farther away from Constantinople. Now resting on the Count of Saint-Gilles and now on Bohémond, critical reproach for the quarrels over Antioch has fallen in point of time as early as the Provençal scouting party from the neighborhood of Coxon. Yet the two appeared to abide by councils in the decisions that governed the army in their capture of Antioch and their subsequent defeat of Kerbogha.

Many examples of personal bravery and brilliant maneuvering of his forces are attributable to Bohémond. Key points of policy frequently appear to be due to the Count of Saint-Gilles—the cooperation of the Genoese, the success of La Mahomerie, which sealed the Bridge Gate, the distribution of alms which assuaged the sufferings of the poor, and the granting of funds which in turn hastened the fall of the city and protected the camps of the crusaders. As these two men continued to bear themselves well in the trying days of their imprisonment in Antioch, it is reasonable to suppose that whatever their personal aspirations might have been, their conduct in the capture of the city and in the defeat of Kerbogha was one of cooperation for the common cause. It further appears that the rivalry of Bohémond and Raymond at this period has been enhanced by subsequent events. It would be later that Bohémond would push for possession of Antioch, after Alexius' retreat became common knowledge and could be used for purposes of propaganda and personal gain.[12]

NOTES

1. Raymond d'Aguilers, *op. cit.,* pp. 240–41; Fulcher, *op. cit.,* pp. 334–35; Albert, *op. cit.,* p. 329; *Gesta,* pp. 42–56. The author of the *Gesta* and Fulcher offer contradictory versions of the role of Adhémar. We prefer to accept the account of the *Gesta* in view of the corroborative account of Raymond d'Aguilers. Runciman, *op. cit.,* pp. 188 89.

2. The date of Raymond's illness is uncertain. Hagenmeyer has interpreted Raymond d'Aguilers' statement, "usque Antiochiam venimus" to mean Antioch of Pisidia. On the count's illness, see note 13, chapter II, above. It is to be noticed that Raymond's illness is associated with the chaplain's incorporation of materials of a miraculous or moral nature. In this instance he has concluded an episode of miraculous intervention (*Liber secundus Machabaeorum,* X:29–31) and is preparing to relate another (*Isaiah* XXXVIII:1–6). Raymond d'Aguilers, *op. cit.,* p. 241; *Gesta,* pp. 56–62; R. L. Nicholson, *Tancred,* p. 41; Yewdale, *op. cit.,* p. 49. We are not sure of the underlying motives which prompted the expedition into Cilicia and can only note the general effect of it in setting a pattern for the creation of Latin states.

3. *Gesta,* p. 62; Yewdale, *op. cit.,* p. 50. Although one notes increasing tension between Greeks and Latins at this time, there is no proof that Bohémond and Raymond had an open break. Raymond was con-

sistent in the use of councils to decide crusading questions and was consistent in abiding by their decisions. In view of his record, the charge of Yewdale and his successors seems to be based on later examples of the Provençal-Norman feud. The silence of Raymond d'Aguilers on this event leaves us with the brief account of the author of the *Gesta*. René Dussaud, *Topographie historique de la Syrie antique et médiévale,* pp. 167, 171. Dussaud believes that it was customary for Frankish leaders to reconnoiter before advancing. He also calls attention to the fact that problems of military strategy in the crusade are often minimized.

4. Fulcher, *op. cit.,* p. 337; *Gesta,* p. 66. Although Albert was not an eyewitness, his work carries information which reflects general knowledge. See Albert, *op. cit.,* pp. 358–80.

5. Raymond d'Aguilers, *op. cit.,* pp. 241–42; Runciman, *op. cit.,* p. 217. "At alii de principibus in quibus erat comes, dicebant: Per Dei inspirationem nos venisse; per ipsius misericordiam nos Nicaeam munitissimam urbem, obtinuisse; atque per ejusdem clementiam, victoriam et securitatem de Turcis habuisse."

6. Raymond d'Aguilers, *op. cit.,* p. 243; William of Tyre, *op. cit.,* pp. 175–76; Ralph of Caen, *op. cit.,* pp. 649–50; Dussaud, *op. cit.,* discusses the problem of these place names at length, and we have followed Kenneth M. Setton, ed., *A History of the Crusades,* in the location of these towns. See map p. 306, although we are inclined to believe that Ralph's information may be misleading.

7. Cafarus, *op. cit.,* p. 51; Raymond d'Aguilers, *op. cit.,* pp. 243–45; *Gesta,* pp. 66–76; Saint Ambrose, *De Officiis Ministrorum,* in *MPL,* XVI, 88; *Breviarum Romanum,* pars autumnalis, p. 306.

8. Raymond d'Aguilers, *op. cit.,* pp. 245–47; *Gesta,* pp. 76–82; Henri Delpech, *La tactique au XIIIe siècle,* II, 161–66.

9. Raymond d'Aguilers, *op. cit.,* pp. 248–50; *Gesta,* pp. 84–96; Comte Paul Riant, *Expéditions et pèlerinages des Scandinaves en Terre Sainte au temps des croisades,* p. 138.

10. Raymond d'Aguilers, *op. cit.,* p. 250; *Gesta,* pp. 98–102; Kamal ad-Dīn, *Extraits de l'histoire d'Alep,* in *RHC Or.,* III, 580.

11. Raymond d'Aguilers, *op. cit.,* p. 246; *The Alexiad,* pp. 267–78; Chalandon, *op. cit.* ("Essai"), pp. 200–202; Yewdale, *op. cit.,* pp. 58–62. There are many continuators of Chalandon. Krey, *op. cit.* (*Munro Essays*), pp. 75–76.

12. *Gesta,* pp. 100–108; Raymond d' Aguilers, *op. cit.,* pp. 251–53.

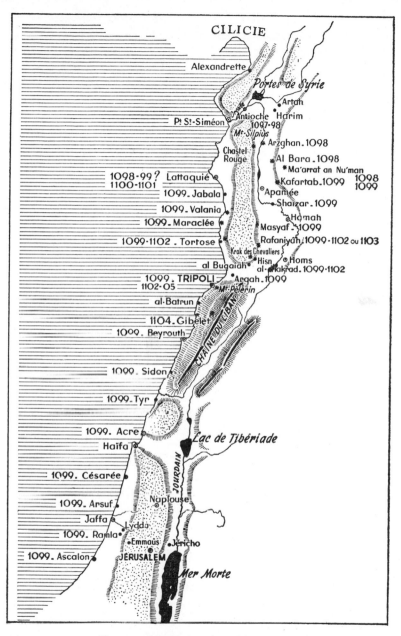

Raymond IV in Syria and Palestine

V

THE NORMAN-PROVENÇAL FEUD

LITTLE TIME remained for the weary Latins to shock the good chaplain, Raymond d'Aguilers, as they whiled away the hours watching pagan dancing girls. The task of fortifying the city, burying the dead, and restoring the church challenged their best efforts. Defense of the east gate, formerly guarded by Bohémond, was entrusted to Godfrey. The castle of La Mahomerie, originally manned by Raymond, was shifted to the count of Flanders and some five hundred men. Raymond now occupied the palace of Yaghi Siyan and protected the Gate of the Bridge. In the early stage of the defense, it seems that Raymond and Bohémond worked together, for we are informed that the two decided to erect a wall and a ditch to prevent sallies from the citadel.

. As the Turkish armies approached Antioch, Godfrey's men were forced to abandon their redoubt, and the outlet of the Iron Bridge was blocked. Shams-ad-Daulah hurried to enlist the aid of Kerbogha in the use of his stronghold as a springboard for an attack on the besieged Christians, but the atabeg of Mosul installed a trusted lieutenant, Ahmad ibn-Marwān, in the citadel to replace Yaghi Siyan's son. Soon he launched an attack from the heights of the citadel, but crusaders met the crush of the Turkish assaults and pressed their infidel enemies back to the stronghold. This costly sortie caused Kerbogha to surround Antioch and attempt a siege of attrition. To the northwest the castle of La Mahomerie fell to the besiegers after a spirited defense by the forces of the count of Flanders. Caught in a pincer attack, crusaders were beset by sneak raids on the towers. Three knights from Malines won the attention of the army by their bravery in blocking one of these attempts.

In such straitened circumstances Christians began to suffer; Antioch had been drained of food by the protracted siege of the past months. Now besieged and cut off from outside supplies, the crusaders sought sustenance where they could find it. Leaves of fig trees, grapevines, and thistles, as well as dried skins of horses, camels, asses, and cattle, were boiled for nourishment. Profiteers prospered as prices rose. Once-proud knights begged for food along with the poor. Raymond and Adhémar became ill, and Bohémond took advantage of adversity to press for control of command. Raymond d'Aguilers reports that all promised obedience to the Norman for fifteen days after the battle. In any case, Bohémond conducted himself as though he were supreme commander. After one raid of the Turks, he set fire to houses near the palace of Yaghi Siyan in order, so states the *Gesta*, to drive crusaders out of hiding. It has been suggested that the violent act was probably prompted by a desire to clear the walls of potential traps which would make defense in the area difficult.[1]

As good fortune deserted the Christians, William and Aubrey of Grand Mesnil and Lambert the Pauper led the rope dancers from the walls of Antioch and slipped through the Turkish lines to the port of Saint Simeon, where they warned the Christian fleet of the plight of their comrades. Here they hurriedly embarked for Tarsus. Closely following them, forces of Kerbogha captured those who remained behind and also blocked the port. Meanwhile, Stephen of Blois, who had retreated to the safety of Alexandretta, heard of his fellow Christians' new difficulties. The author of the *Gesta* tells us that he sneaked back to view from a near-by mountain countless tents of the Turkish horde surrounding Antioch. He fled again and, in company with other refugees from the Christian army, hastened to the emperor with news that all was lost. Alexius and his forces had encamped near Philomelium, and there on June 20 the basileus decided to withdraw his troops. His daughter Anna relates that he was frightened by news of the approach of a strong army of Turks under the command of Ishmael, son of the sultan of Bagdad, as well as by reports of Stephen, in whom he had placed great confidence. Laying down a scorched-earth retreat, Alexius hastened toward Constantinople and left his Latin allies to their fate. As the emperor and his army drew off to the north, the besieged peered from their walls hoping and praying that Greeks would come to their aid.[2]

While crusaders moaned over their unhappy fate and sought means of self-preservation, a Provençal peasant brought tales of miraculous visions to Adhémar and Raymond. Little is known of Peter Bartholomew. Meagre details of his life are furnished by his bitter critic, Ralph of Caen, who only dealt in hearsay. Raymond d'Aguilers has preserved an extended account of these visions. As the chaplain's version goes, the first revelation occurred during an earthquake, probably December 30, 1097, when two men appeared to Peter as he lay upon the trembling ground. The older of the two, after criticizing Adhémar for neglecting his preaching, led Peter Bartholomew into the besieged city, where he conducted him to the church of Saint Peter. Here he revealed the lance which had pierced the side of Christ. As the weeping Provençal mumbled that he would carry it to the Count of Toulouse, his heavenly visitor, Saint Andrew, buried the lance and remarked that it would be found by twelve men who would come to seek it after the city had fallen to the crusading army. Upon his return to camp, Peter hesitated to impart this information to the chieftains because of his lowly estate.

Again, on February 10, 1098, while Peter Bartholomew was in a castle near Edessa, Saint Andrew appeared with his companion and warned him to carry his message to the crusading leaders. Saint Andrew reminded him that he was chosen from all people to execute his command, only to have his order ignored. Then, confronted with failing eyesight, Peter returned to the siege but was again deterred by contemplation of his peasant rank. Welcome relief came when he accompanied his master, William Peter, to the port of Saint Simeon; however, here on March 20 Saint Andrew and his companion appeared to him and upbraided him for not carrying out his instructions. The saint further instructed him to tell the Count of Toulouse to cross the Jordan River, dress in linen shirt and breeches, and be sprinkled with water from the river. The count was then to dry his clothes and lay them away with the Holy Lance. William Peter also heard the words of Saint Andrew, but unlike his servant he could not see the apostle.

Peter Bartholomew returned shortly to the army but was unsuccessful in contacting Raymond and Adhémar. He then journeyed to Mamistra with the expectation of sailing to Cyprus. Here Saint Andrew warned him to return and reveal his message. Ignoring his words, the Provençal peasant attempted three times to sail for Cyprus, only to be driven back each time by violent winds. Properly chastened by these reverses, he returned to Antioch after having undergone a serious illness. Here he was caught in battle and almost crushed to death by horsemen. As he sat dejectedly contemplating his fate, Saint Andrew appeared to him and warned him to carry his messages to the leaders. He then hastened to the tents of Raymond and Adhémar.

The bishop of Le Puy at first doubted the word of Peter Bartholomew and so incurred the enmity of Raymond d'Aguilers. The Count of Toulouse, however, accepted Peter's story and ordered his chaplain to take care of the Provençal mystic. Not to be outdone by a peasant, the priest Stephen recounted one of his own visions. While he was praying in the church of Saint Mary, Christ had appeared to him. At first unaware of the identity of his visitor, Stephen closely observed the beautiful stranger. As he noticed a cruciform light over his head, the priest with wonder and amazement realized that he gazed upon his Lord. In reply to Christ's query concerning the leader of the Christian army, Stephen related that they had no one lord but that Adhémar was trusted more than the others. While the Lord gave Stephen instructions, the Virgin Mary and Saint Peter, according to the *Gesta*, interceded in behalf of the Christians, as was customary in church lore. None of Stephen's companions awakened in time to see the vision. Adhémar ordered that the Gospel and the Cross be brought so that the priest could take an oath that his story was true. At this opportune time, chieftains swore that they would not abandon the siege.[3]

While the briefer version in the *Gesta* is similar to the chaplain's account, the author reverses the order by describing the vision of a certain priest and then that of a pilgrim named Peter. Raymond d'Aguilers devotes more attention to the reporting of revelations from the peasant, whom he labels Provençal. In such circumstances it is hazardous to assign any but a general period as a time for these supernatural visitations. Practical matters were not abandoned, and in the course of this outbreak of miraculous manifestations Bohémond and Adhémar shut the gates of the city to prevent the faint-hearted from abandoning the siege. As the masses awaited the sign of help which Saint Andrew had promised, a meteor lighted the sky and appeared to break into pieces over the Turkish camp. On the following morning, June 14, Provençal leaders heeded the request of Peter Bartholomew and undertook a search for the Holy Lance.

To accomplish the quest an inner circle of trusted Provençals, Raymond of Saint-Gilles, the bishop of Orange, Pontius of Bala-zun, Farald of Thouars, the chaplain, and others, supervised the digging in the church of Saint Peter. Raymond d'Aguilers relates that there were twelve present, while the *Gesta,* without naming them, numbered them as thirteen. The discrepancy in number is explained in that the chaplain did not count the Provençal mystic among the twelve, thus arriving at the number of the twelve apostles. At vespers, after the Count of Toulouse had departed, Peter Bartholomew jumped into the excavation and produced the Holy Lance. The chaplain records later that he kissed the point of the lance as it was uncovered but still lay in the ground.

Had there been no division of interests after the defeat of Kerbogha, the revelation of the Holy Lance would perhaps not enjoy its prominence today. If this is not the explanation of the critical tempest surrounding the miracle, possibly we may find it in man's love of the mysterious and his desire to explore or explode what he cannot understand. In such a medium we have little to guide us, and we are hampered by a certain modern skepticism of our own. On-the-spot reporting, however, agrees that the army was heartened and brought to victory through the miracle of the revelation of the Holy Lance. At the time of its discovery, possession of Antioch was a minor consideration. What was at stake was existence itself. In such circumstances the count, at the sanction of the clerics, gave wholehearted support to this manifestation of divine intervention in the hopeless condition of the army at Antioch; and after his initial hesitation, reported only by Raymond d'Aguilers, so did the bishop of Le Puy. So apparently did the other leaders. The *Gesta* reports that Bohémond, after the priest's revelation of promised aid, was the first of the leaders to take an oath not to flee from the city, and that in this he was followed by Raymond, Robert of Normandy, Duke Godfrey, and the count of Flanders. The appeal of the relic was at first universal, and the Provençal connection was not emphasized among those present except by the chaplain, who may have expressed a later view.

Apparently, when the miracle became suspect it was popularly labeled Provençal, and so became the butt of Norman propaganda and disparagement. Later Latin sources scoffed at the miracles, as did the Saracen writers. They believed that Peter Bartholomew hid the lance, directed the search party to dig, and revealed the relic in the dim light of the church. Some thought that he produced the illusion of unearthing the relic through sleight of hand. Ralph of Caen, who was both absent and anti-Provençal, exaggerated the skepticism of the bishop of Le Puy. Raymond of Saint-Gilles, in the light of such statements, has been charged with exploiting a hoax for purposes of self-aggrandizement.

At the time of the revelation there was no particular reason to question it. It was proper and according to the best tradition that a group identified with a holy cause would have help from the Lord and that this aid should be made manifest through His saints. In pursuance of this idea, the people of the Lord in their pilgrimage on earth were daily surrounded by both the hosts of heaven and those of hell. As objects of attack by evil, they must look for help from the good. That this good was present, and might even manifest itself concretely, was ever a possibility. It was the place of the churchmen to test the authenticity of such manifestations and make decisions as to their truth. With such sanction laymen need have no further doubts.

With these considerations in mind, we can scarcely attribute promulgation of the original story to any but a church group.

The author of the *Gesta* and Raymond d'Aguilers follow the same general pattern in their presentation of the miracle itself and the consequent spiritual preparation of the army for its great battle with the besieging Turks. The extension and amplification of the visions seem to be the work of Raymond d'Aguilers, who here exhibits that he was not under the control of the Count of Toulouse. Apparently familiar with hagiographical proprieties, he was capable of dressing the vision appropriately and extracting from it infinite moral reflections upon the conduct of the army, its leaders, and its accomplishments. In so doing he becomes the voice of the Holy Lance, and the pronouncements of the saints inherit from him the homiletic myopia of a bookish priest.

In the course of his narrative he reveals a certain clairvoyance, exhibits the literary device of allowing coming events to cast their shadows before, and embellishes his thread of crusading history with matters familiar to martyrologies. The chaplain, in extending the miracle of the Holy Lance, used its similarity to Maccabean material with which he was familiar to anticipate events of the crusade and to give the expedition an apocalyptic tone. As Jeremiah gave to Judas Maccabeus a sword of gold to save Jerusalem, the Sanctuary, and the Temple; so in Antioch, while Adhémar yet lived, the Holy Lance as a symbol of leadership was presented to the Count of Toulouse, although the count was not spoken of as a leader until after he left Ma'arrat-an-Nu'mān months later. A Gospel of the Blessed Peter is quoted to link the discovery of the relic with the Christians' subsequent conquest of Jerusalem: "in Evangelio beati Petri est scriptum, quod gens Christianorum quae capiet Iherusalem, infra Antiochiam clausa erit; nec inde exire poterit, nisi prius lanceam Domini repererit." In shaping his visions the chaplain uses the customary device of the simple man hesitant to divulge his experiences. Vainglorious in his learning, the chaplain enlarges on the simplicity of the peasant by a patristic device. Saint Andrew's companion is unknown to the peasant, although we are immediately apprised of his identity through the words of the psalmist, "Speciosus forma prae filiis hominum." Saint Augustine has asked who may be so untaught as not to know that this psalm refers to Christ. The answer, according to the chaplain, is Peter Bartholomew, who could through divine inspiration act as a means of communication between the leaders of the army and the heavens above but who could not comprehend the matter of his own vision. He had to be told by Saint Andrew that the apostle's companion was the Lord Jesus Christ.[4]

Regardless of the source of the miracle, the discovery of the Holy Lance produced great joy in camp. Two days after the revelation Peter Bartholomew reported that Saint Andrew, accompanied by Christ, appeared to him with instructions that Raymond should be standard-bearer of the army. This information from the pen of the chaplain presumably corrected his earlier report of the plight of the crusaders, who found themselves in an unfriendly land without one lord as leader. Saint Andrew further instructed Christians to celebrate each year the finding of the lance. Crusaders were to conduct themselves as taught in the Epistle of Peter, "Humble yourselves under the mighty hand of God." Clerics should sing before the Holy Lance, "Lustra sex qui jam peracta tempus implens corporis." Raymond d'Aguilers adds corroborative detail, relating that he and the bishop of Orange interrogated Peter and found that he knew the *Pater Noster, Credo in Deum, Magnificat, Gloria in excelsis Deo,* and the *Benedictus Dominus Deus Israel.* To the chaplain this was indeed little learning, and the evidence is used to underscore the divine inspiration of the utterances of a poor peasant whom it is doubtful that the devil wanted in hell.

Saint Andrew returned again with instructions. Crusaders were to give alms for the five wounds of Christ or say the *Pater Noster* five times. The battle cry was to be "God help us!" The apostle promised victory but warned against the search for gold and silver as spoils of battle. Thus, as the battle neared and the apostle became more practical in his instructions, activity in preparation for defeating the enemy came from forces other than celestial. Apparently Bohémond called a council which resulted in the dispatch on June 27 of an embassy, composed of Peter the Hermit and a Christian named Herluin, to treat with Kerbogha. Although no terms of surrender satisfactory to the besieged were arranged, it is possible, as some have suggested, that emissaries learned the forces of the governor of Mosul had dwindled. The crusaders now decided to fight an offensive battle, and after three days of prayers and processions they were psychologically prepared to turn upon their besiegers.

On June 28 in the early morning trumpeters went through Antioch arousing the people and telling them to stay within the ranks of their leaders. The army divided into six ranks under the command of Hugh of Vermandois and Robert of Flanders, Godfrey, Robert of Normandy, Adhémar, Tancred and Bohémond, in the order named. Provençal forces were divided. Raymond of Saint-Gilles remained in Antioch with two hundred followers to guard the citadel and prevent an attack from the rear. Raymond d'Aguilers reports serious illness as the reason for this assignment; however, it is not likely that such an important assignment would be given to a man as gravely ill as the chaplain represents.

The main force of the Provençals, under the command of Adhémar, bore the brunt of Kerbogha's attack. The author of the *Gesta* states that the bishop of Le Puy carried the Holy Lance while Raymond d'Aguilers asserts that he himself carried the relic. Later accounts attribute the carrying of the lance to Adhémar, despite reports that he doubted its validity. Other Provençal leaders, Isoard, Count of Die, Raymond Pilet, Gaston of Béarn, Gérard of Roussillon, William Amanieu, and William of Montpellier, fought in a separate unit, perhaps with the near-by Normans. Thus, in this battle, as well as in previous actions, Provençals followed Norman leadership, petty grievances were forgotten, and there was no sign of the later Norman-Provençal quarrel.

Kerbogha, in the meantime, planned to allow the whole army to march outside of Antioch before he attacked and made an end of the troublesome Christians. Fanciful though the account may be of his playing chess while the Frankish units assembled outside the walls, it may well express the stupidity of his decision. He may have gauged well their starving condition, but he reckoned without the intensity of their inspiration. Priests in white vestments walked with bare feet upon the walls holding their crosses and blessing the army as it moved with new-found dedication from the Gate of the Bridge. With tattered standards and scrawny steeds, the soldiers of Christ rattled their arms, brandished their spears, and arrayed their lines outside the city.

The sight frightened the atabeg of Mosul, who now proposed to discuss a truce. The offer was ill-timed, and, failing to gain a peaceful settlement, Kerbogha turned to tactics of withdrawing his troops so that they could resort to wheeling movements which would envelop the flanks of the Christian army. Rainald of Toul met the flanking attack from the left, and held. While this diversionary maneuver was going on, Provençals under Adhémar bore the brunt of the Turkish onslaught. In the melee Heraclius, standard-bearer of the bishop of Le Puy, was wounded. Other units of the Christian army, continuing to harass the Turks, relieved the hard pressed forces of Adhémar. The united stand of the soldiers of the Cross caused the allies of Kerbogha to waver. Dukak fled and panic spread as did the grass fire which Kerbogha had set to delay the Christian attack. Soon the battle-field was turned into a rout with the atabeg of Mosul leading a wild flight, urged on by revengeful Christians in hot pursuit. The militia of Christ hacked and slew the Turkish footmen as far as the Iron Bridge, and many of those who escaped fell victim to treacherous Armenians and Syrians.

As the deeds of men made history on that day, so did the miracles. The author of the *Gesta* apportions celestial aid impartially. In his account, the bishop carried the lance in battle, an act which belied the seriousness of his reported skepticism; the army of the saints appeared from the mountains, as the psalmist has it, "whence cometh our help"; and names from the calendars of the West, Saint George, Saint Mercurius, and Saint Demetrius, were attributed to its leaders. The chaplain, who could usually see celestial intervention as quickly as anyone, did not write of the appearance of the heavenly leaders; however, he mentions that priests in white garments were present and that the crusading army was so multiplied by God that it outnumbered the enemy. He further attributed the success of Adhémar's army to the saving power of the lance. Even Heraclius, the standard-bearer of the bishop of Le Puy, would have been saved, had he not strayed from the relic's protection. With the work of battle done, crusaders, having followed Saint Andrew's practical instructions not to pillage until the battle was won, could now take gold, silver, grain, wine, butter, and livestock which the Turks had left in their haste.

Meanwhile, the commander of the garrison, Ahmad ibn-Marwān, offered to surrender to Raymond of Saint-Gilles, who had watched the citadel during the battle beyond the walls. Raymond d'Aguilers relates that some of the garrison surrendered, while others fled and were killed by the Christians, an observation reinforced by Moslem sources. He further informs us that the citadel was afterward occupied by the men of Godfrey, Robert of Flanders, Raymond of Saint-Gilles, and Bohémond, thereby witnessing the character of joint effort in preserving the city from the peril of counterattack. The author of the *Gesta,* however, would not have it so, and informs us that Ahmad ibn-Marwān reversed his decision to surrender to the Count of Toulouse and surrendered to Bohémond, a statement which does not account for the presence of the combined forces in the citadel after the rout of Kerbogha.[5]

The sequence of events following the defeat of Kerbogha is obscure. Later writers are biased by subsequent developments, and both the *Gesta* and Raymond d'Aguilers exhibit points of view influenced by quarrels of the summer and fall. On the surface, Latins and Greeks cooperated in efforts to restore the shrines, which had been desecrated in Antioch by the Turks. Crusaders, probably upon the advice of Adhémar, restored the Greek patriarch John to his see in Antioch and from a common fund aided the Greek clergy in restoring the services of the church. In the first few days of July, crusaders sent Hugh of Vermandois and Baldwin of Hainault to inform Alexius of the defeat of the Selchükids and perhaps to secure aid of the basileus for continuation of the expedition. One may infer that the influence of Adhémar and Raymond prevailed here, for the dispatch of such a mission was in accord with their previous policies and could only anticipate the arrival of the Byzantine ruler and his assumption of dominion in Antioch, as most of the crusading leaders had promised by their oaths at Constantinople. On July 3, 1098, chiefs in council decided to postpone the expedition to Jerusalem until November, when cooler weather would make the journey less hazardous. A very difficult siege had been completed only recently, supplies of the region had been plundered by both themselves and the Turks, and the army in its exhausted state was in no condition to undertake the hazards of an expedition into territory reportedly lacking in water and occupied by untried enemies.

We are not told that these actions were displeasing to Bohémond, and the *Gesta* places the departure of the princes (*divisi sunt seniores*) to their own lands here. The chaplain reports the departure of the princes after the death of the bishop of Le Puy and infers that their departure resulted from their quarrels (*inter se divisi principes*). However, the summer activities seemed to have had sanction of an over-all plan. Bohémond exhibited no fear of the Count of Toulouse in absenting himself from Antioch. Heralds went forth in the city to invite the poor to make agreements and find shelter under whatsoever banner they chose; and so affairs were arranged in perfect harmony. What leaders had not perhaps fully appreciated in their planning was the effect of the mortal sin of sloth, a matter which the chaplain and other churchmen understood much better, apparently, than they. Instructed by the blessed Gregory, Raymond d'Aguilers well knew that idleness made the body unhealthy. For the amorphous mass of the army there was nothing to fill the vacuum created by the collapse of the Selchükids, and quarrels shaped themselves into a Norman-Provençal feud. Whereas in the time of peril it had been to the interest of lay and church leaders to smooth over occasional displays of bad blood and sporadic fights between the two forces, comparative safety now allowed other considerations to creep in. Enhanced by alternatives presented in the emperor's retreat, growing unrest among the hungry masses, and the bitter resentment against the Greeks, feuds developed which no one seemed to be able to quell.

Again conflicting chronology does not permit us to say when the disputes attracted attention. During the summer the *Gesta* speaks of happiness in Antioch, and abruptly says that, after the gathering of the princes in the fall, they decided that it was time to cease their quarrels and plan for the resumption of the expedition. The chaplain, on the other hand, leads us to believe that soon after the victory over Kerbogha, Bohémond, as a part of what they later learned was an evil design, drove the men of Godfrey, the Count of Flanders, and the Count of Saint-Gilles from the citadel under the pretext that he had sworn to the Turk who surrendered the city that he would hold it himself. We do not know whether this refers to Fīrūz, who originally betrayed the city, or to the commander of the citadel. The presence of the united forces in the citadel would indicate that there was no such agreement with the surrendering commander. Raymond d'Aguilers continues that Bohémond, in pursuance of his plan, requested the strongholds from the other leaders. The bishop and the duke complied, but the Count of Saint-Gilles would not give up the palace of Yaghi Siyan and the Gate of the Bridge, which his forces had recovered in the course of the fall of the city, and which he had continued to occupy as a part of the defense planning against Kerbogha. The chaplain further informs us that both the bishop and Raymond were ill at this time and unable to protect their men from the arrogant Normans, who openly insulted the helpless Provençals.

Thus the chaplain, who had foreshadowed Bohémond's scheming for the city since early in the year, placed the open quarreling for possessions in Antioch soon after the defeat of Kerbogha and before Adhémar's death. We have evidence that Bohémond was moving secretly during the summer toward support for his claim to the entire city. On July 14, 1098, he made an agreement with the Genoese by which he promised to give them the church of Saint John, a well, some houses, and trade rights and exemptions from tolls and taxes in Antioch. In the event of an attack upon the city, they pledged their aid; however, they reserved the right to remain neutral in the event of a quarrel between Raymond and Bohémond. In their reservations the Genoese seemed to exhibit their knowledge of the situation. Bohémond was unofficially seeking support for his possession of Antioch, which apparently had not been approved by the council of leaders but would come up at their designated meeting in November. That he may have approached other leaders during the summer seems indicated by subsequent reporting of arguments in council; however, we may only surmise through their attitudes in the autumn that Bohémond was unable to place them openly in violation of their pledge to the emperor, even as the Genoese, who were in concord with Raymond, refused to violate their commitments to him. Thus Bohémond sought to isolate the count.[6]

While the army waited for November and the resumption of the expedition, raids into near-by Saracen lands took some of the pressure of idleness off the forces, which were now beginning to suffer for lack of supplies. On July 14, Raymond Pilet, a knight in the army of the Count of Saint-Gilles, made a raid southward into Moslem territory and three days later came to Tel-Mannas, where he was welcomed by the Syrian inhabitants. After a sojourn there of eight days, he captured a near-by castle and put to the sword those occupants who refused to accept Christianity. Provençals then turned to capture Ma'arrat-an-Nu'mān, a Turkish stronghold, but a large force from Aleppo defeated and routed the Christians on July 27. Casualties were very heavy among the undependable poor and the Syrians.

Back in Antioch, Adhémar fell victim to a plague, which had decimated the city, and died on August 1, 1098. His body was buried in the church of Saint Peter of Antioch, as his fellow soldiers in Christ mourned his death. For his later reputation his unexpected demise proved fortunate. Historians have imagined that all would have been well if Adhémar had lived. His death has been termed a disaster by modern writers, who assume that the success of the crusade lay in his conciliatory abilities. Had he lived, he would have faced the problems that the princes faced in their November councils. Bohémond, already gaining support for possession of Antioch while the bishop lived, would scarcely have been turned from his purpose by Adhémar's presence during their arguments in the church of Saint Peter and in subsequent councils. The defection of Alexius at this stage of the crusade was a damaging blow to Latin and Greek friendship. No other period would have tested the bishop of Le Puy so rigorously. But Adhémar dead was a supporter for whatever leader chose his spotless name. Adhémar alive would have had to speak for himself and choose sides in the now well defined quarrel.

Outwardly princes showed no great change immediately after

the death of Adhémar. Bohémond and Tancred strengthened
their holdings in Cilicia. Godfrey, probably accompanied by
Viscount Gaston of Béarn, visited his brother, Baldwin, in Edessa.
Raymond's movements are uncertain, although it appears that
his headquarters for numerous raids was located at Chastel-
Rouge. Modern historians who urge that the Count of Saint-
Gilles planned to seize Antioch forcibly follow Ralph of Caen
and neglect to note that Bohémond, a more astute judge of the
count than we may be, apparently had no fears on this score.
The Norman leader recognized that the question at stake was
the interpretation of their individual commitments to Alexius.
In so doing he could absent himself from his coveted city without
fear of violence from the count.[7]

Quarrels in the council with Bohémond were to wait until
later in the year; not so the Count of Saint-Gilles' troubles with
the churchmen. Adhémar, who won the enmity of some of the
lesser clergy in life, became their repentant ally in death. By
extension of the miraculous content of his narrative, Raymond
d'Aguilers seems to express the dissatisfaction of a group of
Greek-hating clergymen who, independent of the Count of Toulouse, played between the masses and the leaders. At this point,
princes who desired to settle around Antioch and other territories
included in the Greek domain and now won from the dominion
of the Turks, would desire that Alexius remain in the north. In
this they were in accord with the Latin church party, which
feared the Greek clergy would take possession of rights acquired
in captured localities. Leaders who wished to continue the
crusade would see the necessity of help from the basileus in their
further inroads into Saracen lands. This reasoning explains in
part their timidity in accepting Bohémond's demands. The
pilgrims and footmen, since they would have to buy at market
in recovered Greek land, would wish to continue their gainful
occupation of raiding Saracen lands, a pastime they could not
carry on with any safety and profit without support from the
heavily armed knights. Ever a source of danger to the army in
their unruly rapacity and cowardice, this rabble was a responsibility of the Count of Toulouse by virtue of his pledge at Cler-

mont. In seeking to care for them, he was hampered by their superstitions, which made them a tool of the lesser clergy.

Conveniently for the anti-Greek elements, another vision was reported by Peter Bartholomew on the second night after the burial of Adhémar. The good bishop, whose face and head had been singed in the interim for his momentary doubt of the relic, now expressed his belief in the Holy Lance. This punishment, reported by the chaplain, was not original with the bishop of Le Puy. Good men before had received such punishment, according to martyrologies. It expressed the idea that to live is to sin and that the worthy man's punishment was limited. Adhémar stated in this visitation that Raymond should select a bishop to succeed him. The tradition of Adhémar's intervention in church affairs is continued by Ralph of Caen, who later claimed that the bishop of Le Puy selected Arnulf of Chocques to succeed him.[8]

If, at this stage, the visionaries had ended their communications with those who, by virtue of their martyrdom in the crusade, had joined the white-robed saints of the Apocalypse, Raymond's cause would not have been embarrassed. However, the chaplain continued to record more instructions from the bishop in death than he had voiced in life, and in so doing robbed him of the integrity and expressed judgment that we believe him to have possessed. He advised Raymond and Bohémond to bury their grievances, and he urged the count to abandon the cause of the emperor. Thus tacitly suggesting that Antioch be turned over to the Norman, the chaplain declared that Adhémar had further entrusted to Raymond the cause of leading the Christians to Jerusalem. As he conveyed this same notion of the count's leadership in his tale of the visions at Antioch, we can feel that Raymond d'Aguilers is further playing into the hands of Bohémond by advocating a plan that would relieve the Norman chieftain of both the embarrassment of the emperor's coming and the presence of the unruly mass of the army in his city and surrounding lands. He was further revealing the problems of his so-called master, whose commitments to Urban and Alexius would not permit him to follow the path urged by the nearsighted clergy.

In early September absentee leaders returned to Antioch, and on the eleventh of the month Bohémond, Raymond, Godfrey, the count of Flanders, and the count of Normandy wrote a letter to Pope Urban in which they gave an account of the success of the crusading army and in turn suggested that the pope come to Antioch. The postscript of the epistle, lacking from the Vatican manuscript and evidently re-edited by supporters of Bohémond, advised Urban to break with Alexius because he had forsaken his promises. This apocryphal addition seems to have been a part of Norman propaganda to discredit Alexius in the West. It likewise indicates the character of Bohémond's arguments to legalize his seizure of Antioch. Other than the postscript to the letter, the communication seemed to be a formal note for further instructions from Urban to an army that had been deprived by death of the pope's vicar. It underscored the fact that Adhémar did not appoint a successor during his lifetime and that the princes recognized they had no right to do so.

By this time the Count of Toulouse had apparently recovered from his sickness as reported by his chaplain. We again are impressed by the durability of the old warrior and his speedy rebound from what Raymond describes as a serious illness. The count now devoted the next few weeks to raiding Moslem territory, probably in search of supplies. Perhaps on September 14, at the request of Godfrey, he joined forces with him to undertake the relief of a rebellious satrap of 'Azāz, who was besieged by his overlord Ridvan. The scheme proved costly. Although the forces of Ridvan fled upon the news of the approach of crusaders, Provençals lost heavily, perhaps through skirmishes, as they returned to Antioch. This unfortunate experience no doubt emphasized the dangers to come and urged the necessity of unified effort. Both at Ma'arrat-an-Nu'mān and here Turkish forces, whether they remained and fought or turned and fled, were a mobile and ever present peril to undermanned expeditions.[9]

Upon his return Raymond was confronted with a new visitation and demand from Saint Andrew. Raymond d'Aguilers states that the good saint appeared to Peter Bartholomew, who was at Chastel-Rouge with the bishop of Apt, to a chaplain named Simon, and to the author himself. Never reluctant to transmit heavenly communiqués to the old count, Peter stated that Saint

Andrew complained of Raymond's evil counsellors and told him to ignore their advice and hasten to Jerusalem, which would be given to him if his commands were obeyed. The saintly complaints caused Raymond to confess and do penance, lest his works sink like a melted candle into the ground.

Raymond seems to have had a clear notion of the province of the clergy. If he humored them in their conception of sin, he was not trusting them in decisions concerning practical problems involving the Turks. The journey to Jerusalem had to await developments more favorable than visionary. In the meanwhile hungry mouths had to be fed and the count took to the field. On September 25, he set out from Chastel-Rouge with many poor people and a few knights, to make a foraging raid into Moslem territory. In October he besieged Albara, a town southeast of his headquarters. Here Raymond was a ruthless victor, according to his chaplain as well as by the accusations of his enemies. Thousands were killed, many were tortured, perhaps to reveal hiding places of their treasures, others were sold into slavery, and only those who surrendered while the siege continued were permitted to go free. The heavy casualties inflicted upon the enemy are probably exaggerated, because the chaplain has led us to believe that the action was a small raiding expedition, and certainly absence of serious Moslem opposition throws suspicion on his story. More significant is the fact that Raymond made an example of those who defied him and yet opened the door to those who submitted. As a fierce foe respected by the Moslems for keeping his word, he could now expect to receive overtures from Saracen leaders on his way to Jerusalem. Thus he was one of the first to understand the disadvantage of demanding an unconditional surrender. By combining negotiations and force on the road to the Holy Sepulcher, he was to gain more than could have been accomplished through fanatical extermination.

Upon the insistence of the masses, after a council and an inquiry as to whether there was a bishopric already established, the count made Peter, a native of Narbonne, bishop of Albara. Raymond granted Peter half the city and its lands, and it is to be supposed that at the same time he indicated the extent of his bishopric, which according to later developments may have included Ma'arrat-an-Nu'mān. Likewise, the election is significant in that it was a step in the establishment of the Latin church in the East. However, the Greek patriarch consecrated Peter as bishop of Albara. Thus the eastern church was not disregarded, and the Latins were pleased. This assumption of dominion by conquest on the part of the Count of Saint-Gilles indicates what chroniclers had implied concerning certain lands to the south of Antioch. In these lands, distinguished as Saracen, there was no pledge of overlordship to the emperor.[10]

During the months of October and November, 1098, the lesser people of the crusade became more eager for resumption of the march to Jerusalem and resented the controversy at Antioch, which they viewed as the obstacle that blocked the way. The chaplain complains of the quarrels of the leaders and reports threats to throw down the walls of the city, a foreshadowing of the destruction that he would report dramatically at Ma'arrat-an-Nu'mān. Raymond, returning from Albara, attended a church council in the church of Saint Peter on November 5, 1098. The council concerned itself with Bohémond's claims to Antioch and with furthering the expedition to Jerusalem. Godfrey, the count of Flanders, the count of Normandy, and Bohémond were present.

In the course of the arguments in the church of Saint Peter, Bohémond stressed the failure of Alexius to come to the aid of the crusaders and, according to the *Gesta,* reminded the leaders of their promise to entrust the rule of Antioch to him. Whether the author of the *Gesta* refers to individual promises similar to the accord with the Genoese in July or seeks to support here its previous declaration that the princes in council promised the city to Bohémond before its fall in early June, it is not possible to say. Events which follow support further the idea that no such official promise had been made. Certain of the leaders argued that Christian inhabitants would be assured protection of an able military leader if the city were guarded by Bohémond. Raymond could not be led to this point of view. He reminded the council that it was Bohémond who persuaded him to take the oath to the emperor which he himself now demanded that they honor. It has been urged that the Count of Saint-Gilles took no oath to Alexius; however, this point of view was born of failure to grasp the import of the language with which the oath was described. Both the *Gesta* and Raymond d'Aguilers agree that the Count of Toulouse swore to respect the possessions of Alexius. Raymond's position, therefore, was different from that of the other leaders. He was not a vassal or a mercenary. He was sworn to return the emperor's lands to him if he himself recovered them. In this case, the towers and palace in Antioch, held in trust for Alexius, could not be bartered.

Though he sought support now on the basis of the failure of Alexius to help, in later years Bohémond would go to great lengths to avoid the label of perjurer. Recalled to their duty in a conference held in the church of Saint Peter, Godfrey, Robert of Flanders, and Robert of Normandy would not put themselves in perjury by supporting Bohémond in his contentions. In the furor of the argument the leaders all but came to blows. At this point the *Gesta* makes another effort to report the compliance of the Count of Saint-Gilles in an attempt to conciliate the differences but at the same time to obviate the charge of perjury. He reports that in the resulting impasse which prevented the expedition to Jerusalem, Raymond offered to abide by the decision of his peers, preserving, of course, his commitments by oath to the emperor. Bohémond and the Count of Toulouse put their hands in those of the unnamed bishops and promised not to disturb the march to the Holy Sepulcher. This agreement appeared to be little more than a peace of discord, with Bohémond fortifying the citadel and Raymond garrisoning the Tower of the Bridge and the palace of Yaghi Siyan. If this accord is genuine, it is hard to understand why there were yet two occasions more when Bohémond and Raymond would dispute the matter of guarding Antioch. Was this another effort to maintain the consent of the count and to justify the forcible seizure of Raymond's strongholds? The count, of course, was not forsworn if he were overcome by force.[11]

Soon after this council, perhaps November 23, Raymond of Saint-Gilles and, according to the chaplain, Count Robert of Flanders, left Antioch, journeyed to Albara, and then turned south to Ma'arrat-an-Nu'mān, a Moslem town which Raymond

Pilet had attacked unsuccessfully several months before. The
underlying motives for such an attack have been the subject
of many interpretations. Grousset and many others have assumed
that the attack was inspired by Raymond's desire to offset the
growing power of Bohémond. Fulcher, as well as William of
Tyre, states that a council of the crusaders decided to march into
the interior of Syria in order to clear the road to Jerusalem.
Two routes were possible south from Antioch. One was to the
west along the coast, and the other was to the east of the Jabal
Ansārīyah. Apparently in bringing the scattered forces to an
assembly point, the princes decided to use both routes. For
Raymond's forces, which had been south of Antioch in this region
during the summer and fall, the valley of the Orontes was the
logical route to the junction of the two armies in the neighborhood of Tripoli, where the interior forces could conveniently
reach the coast. As Ma'arrat-an-Nu'mān had once defied the
knights of the Count of Saint-Gilles, Bohémond's forces presumably were added to carry this stronghold which would, if by-
passed, menace the crusaders. The assignment, so states Fulcher,
fell to Raymond and Bohémond. Inasmuch as the roster of the
leaders present is at variance in the sources, Kügler has surmised
that the omission of names is a mark of carelessness rather than
an indication of their absence from the siege. If such is the case,
then it may be assumed that the attack was one of general
strategy rather than one of Raymond's efforts to block his Norman
rival.[12]

On November 28 and 29, defenders of Ma'arrat-an-Nu'mān
repelled attacks of the forces of Raymond, which had been
strengthened by the arrival of Bohémond. After the initial
failure of the onslaught, crusaders settled down to siege operations
in which they were handicapped by lack of machines. As early
enthusiasm waned, hunger caused the besiegers to forage for
food. The defending Turks taunted and jeered Christians, blasphemed their God, and desecrated crude crosses which they displayed from the walls.

Aid for the besiegers came from both practical and visionary
fronts. The chaplain reports encouraging news from the bishop
of Orange, who had attempted somewhat feebly to assume the

duties of Adhémar. Calling an assembly, the bishop revealed that there had been a visitation from Saint Andrew and Saint Peter, during which the crusaders were chided for their adultery and oppression. However, the heavenly ones added the consoling news that the town could be taken. Raymond of Saint-Gilles, meanwhile, constructed a movable tower which his men rolled against the walls of the city as Everard the Hunter blew a trumpet loudly and sounded the call to battle. William of Montpellier and many knights in the upper compartment of the tower hurled stones upon the hapless enemy. As the priests in their vestments prayed for victory, Moslems hurled beehives, Greek fire, and lime upon the attackers in the rolling tower. Moslem efforts, however, were fruitless. On December 11, led by Godfrey of Lastours, soldiers of Christ scaled the walls and captured a few towers. As the bloody Sabbath came to an end, Bohémond proclaimed through an interpreter that those who would escape death must enter a palace near by and depend upon his generosity.

On the following day Ma'arrat-an-Nu'mān fell to the Christians. Greedy crusaders tortured Saracens in order that hidden treasures could be located. Frightened people were smoked out of hiding places in caves with sulphur fumes, and those who relied upon the word of Bohémond were either slain or sold into slavery. The timid dashed themselves to death in cisterns, but even death failed to deter the *militia Christi,* who cut open bodies of the dead to recover coins which had been swallowed in desperate efforts to retain worldly goods.[13]

Before the streets were cleared of the dead, the feud of the Normans and the Provençals flared again. Bohémond, who had played a relatively inconspicuous part in the siege, now began to seize the lion's share of the booty. He refused to relinquish some of his towers, and for a time it appeared that he would not recognize Peter of Albara's right to guard the city. Disaster and famine as usual followed victory. The bishop of Orange fell victim to disease, and further weakened the influence of the higher clergy by his untimely death. Morale in the ranks was extremely low, and Christians resorted to cannibalism. With affairs in this dismal state at Ma'arrat-an-Nu'mān, the masses clamored for the only remedy they knew—further penetration of the unplundered lands, an activity which they linked with the resumption of the march to Jerusalem.

Bohémond and Raymond held a meeting in the newly captured town on December 29. Bohémond suggested that they delay departure until Easter. Others added that with Godfrey absent it was dangerous to resume the march at this time, as the small number of knights and horses made such a venture hazardous. In the meanwhile, according to Raymond d'Aguilers, the bishop of Albara and a few nobles met with the lesser people and summoned Raymond to them. They besought him to lead them to Jerusalem. If he failed them in this, he could give them the Holy Lance, and they would resume the journey with its protection. Here the Provençal leader was caught at a loss for a practical solution of the problem of conflicting interests. He well understood that other leaders might not join him if he set the date of departure without consulting the council. The masses, he also knew, could neither survive nor capture Jerusalem without the knights. The lesser clergymen were too impractical to recognize that they played upon the superstitious predilections of foot soldiers and pilgrims to reduce a singularly successful expedition to the status of a peasants' crusade, which could only expect another such slaughter as had been dealt the hapless horde under Peter the Hermit.

In this situation the Count of Toulouse played for time. He promised that he would lead the pilgrims to Jerusalem, and at the same time he summoned leaders to Chastel-Rouge for a council. Meanwhile, Bohémond, incensed over proceedings at Ma'arrat-an-Nu'mān, had returned to Antioch; however, he rejoined other leaders in the council of January 4, 1099, and in company with Godfrey, Count Robert of Normandy, and Robert of Flanders listened to Raymond's plea to continue the crusade. Bohémond again refused to follow the plans of the Count of Saint-Gilles for resumption of the march to Jerusalem unless he received possession of Antioch. His action in this matter leads us to wonder if the author of the *Gesta* was correct in his report of the previous accord at Antioch. Raymond, on the grounds of his oath to the emperor, continued to oppose Bohémond's

demands. Other leaders apparently backed Bohémond and refused to follow Raymond's counsel on what appeared to be flimsy
excuses.

To offset their reluctance, the Count of Saint-Gilles offered
ten thousand sous each to Godfrey and the count of Normandy,
six thousand sous to the count of Flanders, and five thousand
sous to Tancred. Perhaps, as some have suggested, the fixed
sums represented the relative importance of these leaders. Viewed
from the standpoint of the history of the expedition, we believe
the offer was accepted. Tancred and the count of Normandy
were to join the army of the Provençals with their knights, and
it would be a relatively short time before Godfrey and the count
of Flanders would make a junction with the army of Raymond.[14]

On the other hand, the impatient pilgrims had little sympathy
with words. While the leaders talked and made plans for the
future conduct of the army, the masses impatiently awaited the
order to march. In Ma'arrat-an-Nu'mān news circulated that
Raymond of Saint-Gilles planned to garrison the town and to
delay the journey. As the rumors spread, according to Raymond
d'Aguilers, an excited mob set about throwing down the walls
of the city. Joined by the weak and ailing, the strong and the
infirm miraculously hurled huge stones from the fortification.
Neither the pleas of the bishop of Albara nor the anger of the
count prevailed upon them. The Count of Saint-Gilles, faced
with undisciplined masses and broken walls, bowed to what he
no doubt felt was the will of God and ordered the remaining
walls to be demolished.

We can wonder, in the light of Fulcher's brief statement that
they sacked the town, the silence of the Gesta, and the chaplain's
later remark that they burned Ma'arrat-an-Nu'mān when they
left, if the count did not warn other Saracen towns of what they
might expect if they resisted his march to Jerusalem. The chaplain, who displays a penchant for seeing fulfilment of ancient
prophecies in the course of the crusade, may as a consequence
have conceived in the action an excuse to incorporate patristic
concepts of Ezekiel 38. Morally, the walls of the opponents of the
City of God will fall when fortitudo sermonis ecclesiastici becomes manifest. We are hampered, of course, by lacking the

service books of the canon of Le Puy; however, since he did not
fail to use Maccabean materials earlier in the story, it is likely
that commentaries on Ezekiel were also present in his homiliar-
ium. Turning, as we believe, from this moral digression, the
chaplain tells us that the count, despite protests from some that
his small force of three hundred knights did not permit raids
against the Moslems, proceeded to make a successful sortie which
netted needed supplies. He then informs us that they burned
the city as they left.

Meanwhile, probably on January 7, Bohémond secured Antioch by expelling Provençal forces that Raymond had left to
hold his tower and palace in that city. Decisive action was re-
quired to meet this new threat to the expedition. Eyewitness
accounts describe vividly Raymond's response to the Norman
action. On January 13, 1099, barefooted as a pilgrim and surrounded by churchmen and loyal vassals, the Count of Saint-
Gilles led his small force from the smoldering ruins of Ma'arrat-
an-Nu'mān. This gesture, magnificent as his contemporaries
depict it, must have been calculated, because the shrewd old
soldier surely knew the other leaders would respond to this
reminder of their sworn quest. Nothing in his past life would
lead us to believe that he would have been foolhardy enough to
attempt to storm Jerusalem with so small a force. The clerics
might believe that their foes would melt away as did the foes of
the Maccabees, but the Count of Toulouse had fought many
battles and was well acquainted with the ingredients of victory.[15]

So the crusade was resumed. In trying to evaluate conflicting
reports of witnesses and to apportion critical praise and blame
for interruption of the expedition, we can draw safe conclusions
only from an over-all picture of the action. Those who seek
to argue from isolated incidents may fall either into the *Gesta*'s
pro-Bohémond reporting of the Norman's seizure of Antioch
or into the miracle mongering of the chaplain. Following this
path of isolated incidents, critics have attacked Raymond of
Saint-Gilles on several counts. Constantly suffering for his pro-
Greek attitude, he has been accused of fathering the hoax of
the Holy Lance, all but wrecking the crusade through his
jealousy of Bohémond, scheming to seize Antioch for himself,

and buying support of other chieftains on the crusade to gain leadership of the movement. However, a general view of the action denies such charges. It was Bohémond who remained in Antioch to hold his prize, and it was Raymond who recalled the other leaders to their vows and first resumed the march to Jerusalem.

NOTES

1. Raymond d'Aguilers, *op. cit.*, p. 253; *Gesta*, pp. 114–28; Albert, *op. cit.*, p. 413.

2. Raymond d'Aguilers, *op. cit.*, pp. 256–57; *Gesta*, pp. 126–30; *The Alexiad*, pp. 282–83; Grousset, *op. cit.*, p. 100. Grousset suggests that the failure of Alexius to relieve Antioch meant that Syria would be French rather than Byzantine.

3. Raymond d'Aguilers, *op. cit.*, pp. 253–55. Although the story of the lance was generally recorded, only Raymond uses it as a vehicle for display of homiletic erudition. We believe that the chaplain's account is his own elaboration of a briefer notice concerning the miracle. For a more traditional explanation see Steven Runciman, "The Holy Lance Found At Antioch," in *Analecta Bollandiana*, LXVIII (1950); Ch. Kohler, *Mélanges pour servir a l'histoire de l'Orient latin et des croisades*, pp. 1–26; *Gesta*, pp. 128–30. It was customary for clerks to have reticence in revealing their visions. A clerk in the region of Tours purportedly received four visits from Abraham but would not relate his visions to princes. Alfred Maury, *Croyances et légendes du Moyen Age*, pp. 326, 343. Natural phenomena offered the correct setting for miracles.

4. Raymond d'Aguilers, *op. cit.*, pp. 256–57, 288; *Gesta*, pp. 132–34, 146; Clemens Klein, *Raimund von Aguilers*, pp. 34–96; Ibn al-Athīr, *Extraits de la chronique intitulée Kamel-Altevarykh*, in *RIIC Or.*, I, 194–95; Ralph of Caen, *op. cit.*, pp. 676–77; *Liber Secundus Machabaeorum*, XV:12–17; *Liber Psalmorum*, XLIV:3; Saint Augustine. *De civitate Dei*, XVII, xvi, in *MPL*, 41, 549.

5. Raymond d'Aguilers, *op. cit.*, pp. 257–88; *Gesta*, pp. 146–60, and footnote 5, p. 155. For saints known in the West see *Aelfric's Metrical Lives of Saints*, ed. Walter W. Skeat, in *The Early English Text Society*, OS, LXXXII, 306–319; LXXVI, 64–67; *English Kalendars Before A.D.*

1100, ed. Francis Wormwald, I (Henry Bradshaw Society, 72); Kamāl-ad-Dīn, *op. cit.,* p. 584; *La chanson d'Antioche,* ed. Paulin Paris, II, 206. (Raymond, described as angry when requested to guard the city, is assured by the bishop of Le Puy of the importance of the post.)

6. William of Tyre, *op. cit.,* p. 274; Albert, *op. cit.,* p. 433; *Gesta,* pp. 160–62; and note 3, p. 161; Raymond d'Aguilers, *op. cit.,* p. 262; Chalandon, *op. cit. (Première Croisade),* pp. 230–31; *Kreuzzugsbriefe,* p. 156.

7. *Gesta,* pp. 162–64; Raymond d'Aguilers, *op. cit.,* p. 262; Nicholson, *op. cit.,* p. 72. The raid of Raymond Pilet is taken as evidence of the cupidity of the Count of Toulouse. Chalandon, Yewdale, Bréhier, Runciman, and others have attributed to Adhémar qualities of leadership which probably were exaggerated after his death. See our article previously cited for a summation of Adhémar's contributions and character.

8. Raymond d'Aguilers, *op. cit.,* pp. 262–64; Ralph of Caen, *op. cit.,* p. 673. Ralph devotes space to a deathbed speech of Adhémar in which the good bishop appoined Arnulf as his successor. Ralph likewise uses his history as a vehicle for his classical references as well as for his personal animus.

9. *Kreuzzugsbriefe,* p. 165; Raymond d'Aguilers, *op. cit.,* pp. 264–65.

10. *Gesta,* p. 168, note 3; Raymond d'Aguilers, *op. cit.,* pp. 264–66; William of Tyre, *op. cit.,* p. 289; Kamāl-ad-Dīn, *op. cit.,* p. 586.

11. Albert reveals that the people had lost confidence in Godfrey, Robert of Flanders, and Bohémond. See Albert of Aachen, *op. cit.,* p. 449. "Et facta est dissensio magna in populo, ac subtraxerunt se multi de populo ducis Godefredi, Robert Flandriensis, et Boemundi, quia in responsis et verbis eorum nullam habuere fiduciam ante multum tempus eundi in Iherusalem"; Raymond d'Aguilers, *op. cit.,* pp. 267–68; *Gesta,* p. 170; Yewdale, *op. cit.,* p. 75. Yewdale maintains that Raymond was insincere in his defense of Alexius. This is purely conjectural and does not recognize the oath of Raymond.

12. William of Tyre, *op. cit.,* p. 290; Bernhard Kügler, *Albert von Aachen,* pp. 183–84; Grousset, *op. cit.,* pp. 120–23; Fulcher, *op. cit.,* p. 352.

13. Raymond d'Aguilers, *op. cit.,* pp. 268–70; Kamāl-ad-Dīn, *op. cit.,* pp. 587–88; *Gesta,* pp. 172–78.

14. Raymond d'Aguilers, *op. cit.,* pp. 270–71; *Gesta,* p. 178; Grousset, *op. cit.,* pp. 124–25. Grousset suggests that these financial offers represent Raymond's desire for the crown of Jerusalem. We do not agree with Runciman that the offer was a bribe and that it was not accepted. Runciman, *op. cit.,* pp. 261, 338.

15. Raymond d'Aguilers, *op. cit.*, pp. 271–72; *Gesta*, p. 180. In discussing expeditions in the neighborhood of Antioch, writers distinguished between Christian lands and "terra Saracenorum," "terra paganorum," or "Hispania." The chaplain perhaps could not withstand the strong link of such terms with homiletic ideas, and in the destruction of Ma'arrat-an-Nu'mān saw the fulfilment of ancient prophecies. *Gesta*, pp. 70–71 and note 4, p. 162; *Kreuzzugsbriefe*, pp. 170, 381–82; Rabanus Maurus, "Commentaria in Ezechielem," in *MPL*, CX, 868, 872; Eusebius Hieronymus, "In Ezechielem," in *MPL*, XXV, 253, 313, 315, 364; *Prophetia Ezechielis*, XXVII:13; XXXVIII:1–4, 20; XXXIX:1–6. That the Count of Saint-Gilles knew how to strike the hearts of his pagan adversaries with terror is attested by both Christian and Moslem sources. *La Chanson d'Antioche* leads us to believe that he understood the language of his enemies (I, 135, and note 2, II, 363).

VI

RECOVERY OF THE HOLY
SEPULCHER

RAYMOND OF SAINT-GILLES, accompanied by Tancred, who led a
small number of knights, and a numerous force of foot soldiers,
turned southward from Ma'arrat-an-Nu'mān with his army. In a
leisurely march, one which was designed to give tardy crusaders
time to assemble, Provençals journeyed to Kafartāb. There Count
Robert of Normandy joined their forces on January 14. During
a three-day sojourn at Kafartāb, messengers from the emir of
Shaizar, who had contacted the crusaders while they were in
Ma'arrat-an-Nu'mān, again brought assurances of peace and good
will from their master. What prompted the friendly reception
is a matter of controversy. Raymond and his vassals had been
active in Saracen lands during the past summer, but we do not
know how far south of Antioch the count's influence may have
extended. Raymond d'Aguilers, who fails to record the summer
raids of Raymond Pilet, accounts for the arrogance of those
besieged in Ma'arrat-an-Nu'mān by relating that they had experienced success against the Christians. However, with the fall of
the city, the Count of Toulouse's merciless treatment of the
inhabitants, and his known respect for treaties, Raymond, better
known by the Moslems as Sanjil, could expect to bring many an
emir to terms without strife.

Whether, then, the emir of Shaizar's offer was prompted by
joy over the overthrow of the Selchükid power, fear of suffering
the same fate as Albara and Ma'arrat-an-Nu'mān, or dread of
the Count of Saint-Gilles, his attitude must have been particularly welcome to the crusaders as they moved southward. Having

gladly accepted the emir's friendship, the army nevertheless moved a force to lodge near his possessions. Objecting to their presence, the emir promised the Christians booty, and on January 17 his guides led them across the Orontes. On the next day the Moslem scouts, pursuant to promises, according to the *Gesta,* or inadvertently, as states the chaplain, led the soldiers of Christ into a fertile valley, where they found pasturing herds. The lord of the valley paid tribute in gold and horses, while the invaders remained there for five days enjoying new-found abundance, particularly five thousand head of livestock. Some crusaders, according to the chaplain, spent their acquired wealth in Shaizar and Homs to buy horses for the journey. The author of the *Gesta,* now following the forces of the Count of Saint-Gilles, remarked that the whole army of Christ (*tota Christi milicia*) was greatly refreshed by this good fortune, a remark which seems to indicate that the main army was on the march under Raymond, and consequently the forces expected under Godfrey, the count of Flanders, and Bohémond, who would follow the seacoast route for a junction in the neighborhood of Tripoli, were regarded by him as comparably negligible contingents, probably gathered from scattered crusaders who, for one reason or another, had not been present at the siege of Ma'arrat-an-Nu'mān or who had left the scene before the resumption of the march southward. We do not know what the author of the *Gesta* meant by *tota Christi milicia,* but we are sure that reinforcements overtook the army as far south as Tyre and that the fleet kept in touch with them down the coast to Jaffa. It seems reasonable, then, to suppose that the line of march, and even some sort of time element, was generally established before the departure of the main, and consequently slower, army from Ma'arrat-an-Nu'mān.[1]

Reasoning from this point of view, we can feel that the chaplain, who has been the occasion of much blame for his master in reporting this march, may often be confused in his chronology along the route. His errors are frequent. He does not record the junction of Robert of Normandy with the army at Kafartāb, although he reveals later along the route that Robert of Normandy is present. Somewhere south of Shaizar he reports an argument between Tancred and the count over the route. The count, he relates, wished to go out of his way a little (*paulisper*) *causa Gibelli* or *Zibelli,* as the variant manuscripts record this bit of information. This report furnished an opportunity for Tancred and many other courageous men to hold forth eloquently in Raymond d'Aguilers' account upon the virtues of hastening to Jerusalem, without designating by what means or by what route they would accomplish this desirable objective. Although he records that the count was overruled, shortly afterward we learn from him that the army deserted the Damascus road and followed a route to the sea in order to make contact with their ships. As this route must have been designated earlier in order to rendezvous with the ships, it is hard to accept the chaplain's report of serious difference here.

In addition to reporting an argument between the leaders, the chaplain's terminology has caused confusion among the moderns. Now, to set out for Jabala, as critics have identified the chaplain's *Gibellum,* from somewhere south of Shaizar the army of Christ would have been forced to march across the Jabal Ansārīyah as well as to reverse the order of march, a tour de force that would have involved more effort at this point than Raymond d'Aguilers' *paulisper.* Yet his followers have inferred such geography from the statement and have used this remark of the canon of Le Puy as a basis for accusing Raymond of Saint-Gilles of viewing Jabala from south of Shaizar across the mountains of the Nusairīs with the idea of blocking Bohémond's ambitions in Antioch. We might add that the practical old count seldom took such a circuitous route to reach a desired objective. It may well be that the chaplain, who demonstrates later that he knows precisely where Gibellum (Jabala) is located, availed himself of this Latinization of a local geographical term to foreshadow at this point later quarrels which he would report at 'Arqah.

Certainly, the author of the *Gesta,* who is much more methodical in reporting the line of march, ignored any dispute over the route in the army's southward journey toward Tripoli. The march led them to Masyāf, where they were well received by the local ruler. On January 23 they then entered the pleasant town of Rafanīyah, which had been recently deserted by its frightened inhabitants. For two days they enjoyed olives and the abundant supplies of the ghost town, while they gazed at the foreboding heights of the mountain before them. Their route would lead them over the mountainous terrain into the valley, al-Buqai'ah, and thence to the coast.[2]

Although the author of the *Gesta* does not record the harassment of Raymond's troops by guerrillas, the chaplain informs us that their enemies took advantage of the march, and, we suppose, of the rugged terrain, to despoil the poor who followed the army. Hagenmeyer has assumed that the attack took place on January 25, although we may conclude from the chaplain's account that such attacks were more or less commonplace between Shaizar and Rafanīyah as well. As a result of the Turkish maneuvers, according to the chaplain, Provençals, who had experienced similar attacks when they crossed the wilds of Sclavonia, resorted to their old tactics. They ambushed a few of the unwary enemy and adopted a military order of march with the Count of Toulouse guarding the rear, and Tancred, Count Robert of Normandy, and the bishop of Albara leading the vanguard. As the old count lay in hiding and devised his surprise offensive against pursuing Turks, his chaplain remarks that great happiness prevailed when Turks were slain and their horses confiscated. Thus protecting themselves from enemy attacks, crusaders entered al-Buqai'ah, where they found a castle which has been identified as the later Krak des Chevaliers or Ḥisn al-Akrād.

As the Christians searched for food, they were attacked by Saracens who had taken refuge in the fort. Relying upon a clever ruse, defenders turned loose their cattle and awaited results. True to form, the Christians became preoccupied with booty. In this critical stage the enemy attacked and trapped the Count of Toulouse. His chaplain states that he was never in greater danger in all his life. After successfully evading the Turks who sought to cut off his return to his men, the old warrior called a council, in which he complained of the negligence of his knights and at the same time received assurances of a continued attack on the fort. On the following day fortune again smiled upon the Christians, who found the besieged had abandoned their castle so hastily that even their dead remained unburied.

Here crusaders celebrated the Feast of the Purification of the

Virgin Mary and remained to enjoy for some two weeks the bounty of the land. Criticized for letting the desire for booty dictate his policy of attacking this castle, Raymond has borne modern censure here. However, from a military point of view, the stronghold held great strategic value. It guarded mountain passes and controlled two important routes. Of established value for the crusading states later, it was, as Dussaud has suggested, a bone in the throats of the Moslems. Furthermore, it was well situated as a base of supplies for operations against Homs. For the immediate purposes of Raymond's army, it meant wiping out a trouble spot both for themselves and those who might follow the army along this route. The chaplain suggests that their success at the fortress, whose defenders had been unwilling either to ask for peace or abandon their stronghold, frightened the whole region. From the *Gesta* we later learn that the army returned to the territory for supplies, so we may conclude that the decision of the count was justified in the over-all policy of his southward march.[3]

With a lifetime of success in psychological warfare, Raymond must have known that his recent victories had impressed the Moslem world. In building his kingdom in southern France, he had worked along the principle that success breeds success, and one good battle avoids many future ones. Now at Hisn al-Akrād he lingered while his enemies made friendly advances. Apparently uninformed as to whether the army would turn inland or continue to the sea, both the atabeg of Homs and the emir of Tripoli hastened to send emissaries. These were received on February 4, and perhaps at that time they realized the direction that the crusading march would take. The atabeg of Homs sent gifts, and, perhaps because his lands did not lie in the line of march, he was allowed to conclude a treaty in which he promised not to molest the crusaders. The emir of Tripoli, through whose lands reinforcements under Godfrey and Robert of Flanders must advance, was not to escape so lightly. Messengers from Raymond journeyed to Tripoli, where, in addition to gaining strategic information for the immediate future of the army, they demanded that the emir accept Christianity. We do not know whether this provision was seriously advanced or whether it was put forward as an alternative to wring more concessions from him. Following the conversations, the banner of Raymond flew from the ramparts of the ruler, but Ibn-'Ammār did not turn apostate. The suggestion has been made that the harshness of Raymond's terms indicated his desire to force the hand of Ibn-'Ammār so that he could seize Tripoli. This speculation of Heinrich von Sybel has been so slavishly followed by succeeding historians that the evaluation of the importance of Tripoli to crusading planning has been forgotten.[4]

In taking the Count of Toulouse to task for policies he urged during the months the army lingered in the neighborhood of Tripoli, critics have given great weight to the complaints of Raymond d'Aguilers, who chose this action as a hook upon which to hang his elaborations upon the sins of the siege. Before the besieging of 'Arqah, he informs us, the count enjoyed great popularity. The army was well fed. The Holy Sepulcher was in reach, and the enemy offered little opposition. The chaplain further remarked that his master's name was more than equal to that of any former leader of the army. Ready now to take up the moral aspect of the siege of 'Arqah, the Provençal historian assists the spin of the wheel of fortune and prepares to swing the reputation of the count into the depths. He relates that Raymond's knights returned from Ibn-'Ammār and persuaded him to attack 'Arqah, a fortified city on the route to Tripoli, urging that after a short siege the wealthy emir would pay a large tribute to save his dependency, and so the count's name and popularity suffered among his own people because of the decision, and Saracens came to think less of him.

Turning aside from the plaints of Raymond d'Aguilers, we must realize that the path had to be cleared for the army's reinforcements, which were expected to follow the coastal route from Latakia, and for contact with ships which would supply the army with markets. Thus, a gathering point for the army in the area surrounding Tripoli offered many advantages which apparently were known to the crusading leaders when their plans were laid for the southward march. In addition, the temper of the emir had no doubt been evaluated through maritime contacts as one to be amenable to an impressive show of

force. Properly handled, he might furnish much needed gold
and silver for the march to Jerusalem, as well as secure the rear
as they penetrated farther into Saracen lands.

Thus it was that Raymond of Saint-Gilles led his army to
the walls of 'Arqah, which he besieged from February 14 to May
13. Of all the acts of Raymond, perhaps none has brought him
greater censure from historians than his investment of this town
which controlled the routes to Tripoli, Latakia, and Homs.
Yet few major events in his crusading career are so poorly reported. The author of the *Gesta* has a short, straightforward
account of the events in the siege. Although he is considered
pro-Norman, his work neither criticizes Raymond nor emphasizes
any quarrels between the leaders. The failure of the *Gesta* to
mention the visions and ordeal of Peter Bartholomew confuses
the issue more.

On the other hand, Raymond d'Aguilers, who muddied the
waters by visions and more visions, has been followed by moderns
who even attempt to explain his celestial seances out of their
ecclesiastical setting. His chronology is abominable, and we
wonder how Hagenmeyer and all who follow in his wake could
give credence to the dating of events during the siege. In addition, the chaplain's lack of interest in description of the fighting,
in obvious contrast with his rather detailed account at Antioch,
leads us to conclude that much of the earlier work of the chaplain was related by his informant, whom he names as Pons of
Balazun, and that his own account of 'Arqah, written some years
after the fact, adds no information on the siege that is not given
by the *Gesta*. However, he does use the action as a motif for the
display of his ecclesiastical didacticism.[5]

The siege operations are poorly reported by the witnesses,
and we must content ourselves with the knowledge that if the
purpose of the Christians was to take 'Arqah they failed. If, on
the other hand, they merely used the siege to weaken the authority
of the emir of Tripoli, who was a source of danger to the expedition, and to win tribute, they were eminently successful. On
February 17, Raymond of Turenne and Raymond Pilet, in an
attack which the chaplain fails to describe, captured Tortosa.
On the preceding night they had built many campfires and

tricked the enemy into believing that a large force surrounded them. As a result, the next morning the victors rode without bloodshed into the town and so found booty as well as an excellent port. The emir of Maraclea to the north immediately requested a banner for protection and offered tribute, thus removing a possible source of danger to crusaders coming south from Latakia. That this action of Raymond cleared the coastal route is inadvertently revealed by the chaplain, who informs us that during the siege of 'Arqah their supply ships could put in at both Tortosa and Latakia.

At the beginning of the siege of 'Arqah, the *Gesta* reports a small but very successful raid against Tripoli. In such desultory fighting the Christians turned to foraging and pillaging the hinterland while they awaited reinforcements. After Bohémond's show of force in Antioch, it is likely that many Provençals now rejoined Raymond's army. It also probable that the crusaders in Antioch began to urge Godfrey and Count Robert of Flanders to begin their southward march. Whether these leaders had delayed to assemble new recruits or whether they still sought to secure the presence of Bohémond, we do not know. Bohémond, according to the author of the *Gesta,* did accompany their forces as far as Latakia, where he deserted the contingents of Godfrey and Robert of Flanders to return to Antioch. The other two leaders delayed their march to 'Arqah by laying siege to Jabala on March 2. Their action at this time leads us to believe that, according to prearranged plans, the units which would reunite near Tripoli did not plan to move to Jerusalem until late spring when the weather and crops were favorable.

Meanwhile, news spread in the crusading camp at 'Arqah that the caliph of Bagdad was leading a force to overwhelm the Christians. Acting upon this information after decision in council, Raymond dispatched the bishop of Albara to summon (*mandaret*) aid from Godfrey and Robert of Flanders. The two leaders thereupon hastily negotiated with the ruler of Jabala, who gave them money, horses, mules, and wine in return for their abandonment of the siege. Rushing to relieve their fellow Christians, they found the Provençals enjoying the bounty of the countryside without any Turkish threat. The author of the *Gesta* reports laconically the reaction of Godfrey, Robert, and their men to the absence of Turkish hosts. They merely lodged beyond the river and besieged the town. The chaplain reports envy of the Provençals and arrogance among the princes.

Pursuant to his remarks, critics have accused the Count of Saint-Gilles of tricking his rivals into abandoning the siege of Jabala, and Albert of Aachen went so far as to charge that the count was paid by the ruler of Jabala to lure Godfrey and the Count of Flanders from the town. Although Albert was removed from the scene by time and space, and Saracen sources confirm the chaplain's statement that Moslems spread rumors concerning the approach of such a force, modern historians have been wont to accept this hearsay account of Albert as an explanation of the arrival of the duke and Robert at the siege of 'Arqah. They also overlook the statement in the *Gesta* that tribute of the emir of Jabala was given when the two lifted the investment of the town. It is also doubtful if the Count of Saint-Gilles was displaying at this time a personal interest in Jabala, which as a former Greek town he would have to return to the emperor. Again historians err because they take this later interest in Latakia and Jabala as proof of his motives in the recall of his colleagues in arms from the town.[6]

Raymond of Saint-Gilles, in penetrating Saracen lands, seemed to follow a policy of advance alternating with delay in the neighborhood of rich masters of cities or fertile lands. According to his chaplain, he had rewarded his army thereby, and even the condition of the sick and poor became much improved. However, in the delay before 'Arqah, although the *Gesta* has nothing adverse to say of the siege, posterity has chosen to blame the Count of Toulouse for holding up the march to Jerusalem, asserting that he coveted Tripoli. Basing their conclusions upon the fact that he later marked out this area for the Provençal county of Tripoli, and arming themselves with the grumblings and miracle mongering of the chaplain, they have misinterpreted the actions of the count and damned him for policies which later, in the face of overwhelming odds, led to the success of the expedition.

If we remember that the chaplain understood deadly sin much

better than he did strategy on the higher levels, we will see from materials he uses in support of sloth, pride, and envy that the army, while it lagged at 'Arqah, concerned itself with securing commitments from cities along their line of march. Perhaps in other conferences Tancred, Robert of Flanders, and Godfrey felt that they should have more of the count's Saracen spoils. Perhaps the chaplain enhances these disagreements with quarrels that arose after the capture of Jerusalem and the removal of the Fātimid threat by the battle of Ascalon. He reports that Tancred withdrew from the count and joined Godfrey, and that the church pressed for a tithe to be distributed to the bishops, the priests, and Peter the Hermit, who in turn would distribute alms to the poor.

Envoys of the emperor, the chaplain reports, came into camp, perhaps on April 10 or 11, bringing complaints against Bohémond's seizure of Antioch. They promised that, if the journey were delayed, the basileus would join the crusaders by the time of the Festival of Saint John, and that their master would reward them. The Count of Toulouse, who had consistently held to his friendship with Alexius, reportedly wished to await the coming of Byzantine forces as well as supplies for the march to Jerusalem. The count, in urging this view in council, further argued that they should not lift the siege of 'Arqah, as it would surrender within the month or be captured by force. If they failed, it would lead to new defiance from Turkish garrisons no longer afraid of Christian threats. Other leaders, aware of anti-Greek sentiment in camp, urged that the embassy of Alexius be ignored. As to Raymond's hopes of capturing 'Arqah at this time, we have only the chaplain's word, and in this statement he contradicts his previous declaration that the siege was for the purpose of extracting rich bounty from the emir of Tripoli. Since the investment of the town did supply the army with riches from the emir, we may suppose that the Count of Toulouse was able to hold the crusaders before 'Arqah until his demands were met.

In the course of the council, Raymond urged that if they awaited the emperor he could lead them to Jerusalem and that they could find common leadership under him. Knowing the old count's ability to wage counteroffensives in council, we can suppose that he offered the opposing leaders an extreme proposal which was unacceptable. Certainly, the march was delayed, but plans for its resumption were in the making. The chaplain reports, in this connection, that his master and the other princes inquired from the inhabitants of the region how the march to Jerusalem might be made. The Syrians (Christians living near Tyre) informed Raymond of three possible routes. One went by Damascus, another cut through the mountains of Lebanon, and a third led along the sea after crossing narrow mountain passes. The Syrians suggested the route along the sea because the Gospel of Saint Peter, which was in their possession, prophesied that those who took Jerusalem would pass along the seacoast. The coastal route would have been the favored one in any case because of the possibility of help from friendly ships. There is a further likelihood that the leaders had investigated the attitude of towns along the route. Apparently, the march south, when it did begin, was well planned. Danger spots were known in advance and cleared by knights, and rulers in their path did not molest them.[7]

Another danger to be fathomed at 'Arqah was the Fātimid threat. The chaplain, with little regard for chronology, reveals the presence of their envoys in camp and the threat they posed. Unknown to the crusaders at that time, Alexius had written to the Fātimids disclaiming responsibility for the invasion of their lands. The Fātimid embassy announced that the vizir of Cairo, al-Malik al-Afdal, would permit small groups of Christians to enter the Holy City as pilgrims. Christians, who were hoping to capture Jerusalem, scoffed at the offer and refused to accept any alliance which denied them possession of the Holy Sepulcher. However, the intransigence of the Fātimids was used to advantage. As reported by the *Gesta* in regard to the accord with the emir of Tripoli, and by the chaplain in connection with the count's agreement with the ruler of Acre, the Egyptian threat was used as a trading device. The emirs hurried the crusaders toward their fate with gifts and promises of friendship. In turn, the crusaders received promises of loyalty if they succeeded in the conquest of the Fātimids.

Two other actions are recorded before lifting of the siege.

A punitive raid was undertaken against the emir of Tripoli. The *Gesta* places the foray soon after the arrival of Godfrey and Robert of Flanders at 'Arqah. The chaplain sets it in the third month of the investment, in response to Ibn-'Ammār's independent and scornful attitude born of crusading dissension. Leaving the bishop of Albara to guard the camp before 'Arqah, a group of Christian knights and footmen attacked a strong force of Saracens assembled near the aqueducts of Tripoli. The aroused Christians quenched their thirst for blood by decapitating Saracens, and viewed with delight the sight of floating heads being borne into the city by way of the canals, which flowed red with the blood of the defenders of Tripoli.

Soon after this attack the *Gesta* reports a raid into the rich lands to the east which netted cattle, sheep, asses, and many other animals, including three thousand camels. Then, in summary of the 'Arqah story, the author reports the happy martyrdom of Anselm of Ribemont, William the Picard, and others, the frequent envoys of the ruler of Tripoli, and the princes' decision to make peace with Ibn-'Ammār. He further states that the crusaders decided in council to resume the march because of the new harvest of fruits and grains. Accordingly, they left this fortified town and came to Tripoli, where they stayed for three days, making an accord with the emir, receiving the three hundred pilgrims whom he released to them, collecting the tribute, and taking advantage of the market which he furnished. Ibn-'Ammār further agreed that, if the army could defeat the Fātimids and take Jerusalem, that he would become a Christian and recognize his lands as a gift from them.[8]

The chaplain cannot resume the journey to Jerusalem so simply. As the military operations lagged, he reports that the discontent of the crowd increased. In contrast to the silence of the *Gesta,* Raymond d'Aguilers devotes many lines to well organized accounts of appearances of celestial visitors. Erratic and often confused on the terrestrial front, the chaplain displays remarkable attention to marshaling heavenly affairs. Peter Bartholomew reported that Christ, accompanied by Saint Peter, Saint Andrew, and a third person, appeared to him while he lay in the chapel of the Count of Saint-Gilles. The Lord, so Peter said, criticized those who remained in their tents during the siege; in an obvious thrust at Godfrey and Robert of Flanders, he likened them to Pilate and Judas. Furthermore, the Lord urged Christians to make an attack upon 'Arqah. However, the chaplain reveals that the magic of the Provençal's visions had disappeared. If, as has been asserted, the old count inspired the vision for political reasons, the results were far from successful. Godfrey and his friends became furious when they learned of the trick. Arnulf of Chocques, chaplain of the count of Normandy, questioned the authenticity of the Holy Lance and, when taken to task for his disbelief, replied that Adhémar had also doubted it. The spell of the Holy Lance had been broken, if we can believe the implications in the reporting of the chaplain. In trying to bolster the authenticity and importance of the relic, he has subjected his master to accusations of controlling the utterance of the visionaries for purposes of his own aggrandizement.

Yet we cannot see, in the light of Raymond's crusading planning or his future actions, basis for the charge that the voice of the lance, as re-echoed by the chaplain, represented the count's wishes or best interests. If the count expected to carve a state south of the Byzantine themes, he had already achieved all that personal interest would suggest. The emir of Tripoli flew his banner and had accepted his protection. After the crusade had been completed and the vows achieved, leaders would be free of the corporate character of their quest. For future dismemberment of Saracen possessions, a tenuous *de jure* pretension in the lands of the emir of Tripoli would be easier to support than *de facto* possession as a result of the united efforts of crusading princes. In the light of Raymond's future conquests in the neighborhood of Tripoli, it would seem that routing crusaders through these lands would have been detrimental rather than advantageous.[9]

Continuing his visionary activities, the chaplain, as though to while away a few hours before 'Arqah, brings many witnesses to confront the skeptical Arnulf. Adhémar is recalled to state again his belief in the relic. Arnulf reportedly confessed and promised to do penance. As he failed to do so, Peter Bartholomew, exceedingly angry, offered to submit to proof by fire.

The *Gesta* and one manuscript tradition of Tudebode ignore this action. A variant manuscript devoted less than a dozen words, after reporting the death of Anselm, to the statement that the judgment of the lance, an action witnessed, according to the chaplain, by sixty thousand people, occurred on Friday before Easter. Following Raymond D'Aguilers, we learn that on April 8, 1099, God's decision took place. Replete with detail and miraculous mysteries, the account he sets forth appears to be an answer to propaganda which is later summarized by the absent Ralph of Caen, who is believed to represent Norman prejudice in the recounting of the Norman-Provençal feud. The canon of Le Puy is assiduous in seeing that details of the affair are correct according to ecclesiastical lore. There are the proper number of witnesses —three to correspond to the witnesses against Christ. The Provençal is slightly burned because of his earthly sins. The event is dignified by being held on the Friday of the Lord's wounding with the lance. Although Peter died later as a result of his ordeal, examination showed that it had been from the press and enthusiasm of the crowd.

To give a final flourish to his account of the departure of the army from the environs of Tripoli, the chaplain related that Stephen of Valence had a visitation from the bishop of Le Puy urging him to bring the bishop's cross for the journey. The Count of Saint-Gilles then sent the bishop's brother William Hugh to Latakia to secure the relic for the army. Secondary accounts have almost without exception followed the chaplain's account of the reluctance of the old count, whom he pictures as a tearful warrior, forced from the neighborhood of the Turkish stronghold by the ambitious duke of Lorraine and the excited crowd that wished to burn its tents and resume the journey to Jerusalem when William Hugh returned with the relic. Again before Tripoli, according to Raymond d'Aguilers, the Count of Toulouse tearfully besought the princes to besiege the city. Celestial visitors thereupon appeared to a priest, Peter Desiderius, urging him to warn the Count of Toulouse not to delay the journey to Jerusalem and not to be niggardly in the distribution of alms.[10]

In contrast to the chaplain's highly fanciful account, the author of the *Gesta* tells us that the army remained before Tripoli three days, while they collected fifteen thousand bezants and fifteen horses, as well as making arrangements for an open market. In view of the fact that the outlines of this settlement were familiar to the Provençal historian, as he demonstrates on two occasions, it is difficult to understand why he depicts his master as wishing to break the agreement before the city. As the Count of Saint-Gilles had gone to considerable effort to build up a successful front for dealing with the Moslems in his path to Jerusalem, we can only assume that the chaplain's ignorance of his master's methods, combined with a vivid imagination and an easy conscience, caused him to take liberties with his material to justify the over-all moral purpose of his work.

On May 16, 1099, the crusaders left Tripoli. According to the author of the *Gesta* they marched at night to al-Batrūn and then came to Jubail, the ancient Byblos. From Jubail they went through the narrow mountain passes on the eve of the Ascension, May 19. They feared ambush here, but the knights went ahead and cleared the way, and so they came to Beirut. Raymond d'Aguilers would have it that the Lord inspired the people to march by night from Tripoli against the commands of their leaders, and so on the following day they came to Beirut. Here we find the chaplain in a parallel with the author of the *Gesta*. The anonymous writer gives to us an account of an itinerary that is understandable and credible, while the Provençal writer takes this journey as an occasion to expand his moral material at the expense of historical accuracy. Thus the *Gesta,* as well as giving us reliable information on the march, gives us an insight into the chaplain's capacity to sacrifice accuracy to moral effect.

Following the coastal route, the Christians proceeded to Sidon and Tyre, where they received reinforcements composed of crusaders from Antioch, Edessa, and Latakia. These additional contingents of crusaders indicate that the dilatory actions of Raymond, which his chaplain so morally deplored, were much better understood by the knights than by the churchmen. From Tyre the army passed by a number of towns that either paid tribute or offered no resistance. After leaving Acre, where the chaplain reports an accord with its ruler, perhaps between Haifa and Caesarea, a carrier pigeon fell into their camp, carrying with it a message warning the ruler of Caesarea of their approach. No incident occurred, and Christians continued by way of the coast to Arsuf, where they turned inland to Ramla, which they entered on June 3, 1099, after a reconnaissance party under the count of Flanders had found it deserted. The near-by church of Saint George of Lydda had been burned by Moslems, who feared that its beams might be used to construct siege weapons. Here Christians established a Latin bishopric under the guiding hand of Robert of Rouen. A small garrison was left to protect the new bishop and his see.

In Ramla Christians in council debated their next move. At this late moment, so states the canon of Le Puy, there were some who wanted to go to Egypt rather than to Jerusalem, but their views did not prevail. On June 6, crusaders marched from Ramla and encamped on the same day at Emmaus, a town revered because Christian lore held that it was here that Christ walked with Cleopas. While encamped in Emmaus, the leaders received an embassy from Bethlehem. They requested aid against the Moslems, who, they feared, might take revenge upon the helpless people of their sacred town. Tancred and a hundred knights rushed to aid their fellow Christians.[11]

Meanwhile, news of the proximity of Jerusalem spread through camp, and many of the eager pilgrims set forth at night. In the vanguard rode Gaston of Béarn, who hoped to seize some flocks grazing outside the walls of the Holy City. Overzealous in plundering the near-by countryside, Gaston almost lost his life when a sortie from the city surprised the small band of warriors. Only the timely arrival of Tancred, then returning from a midnight foray to Bethlehem, saved the Christians from disaster.

The dawn of June 7 brought one of the joyful and yet tragic scenes of history. For three years, thousands of Christians had risked life and fortune to gain sight of the Holy Sepulcher. Now perhaps twelve hundred knights and ten to twelve thousand footmen remained to lay siege to Jerusalem. Barefooted pilgrims hastened to gaze upon the city as they cried with joy while the ever realistic knights began to forage and to seize near-by strongholds. In retrospect William of Tyre could exhort along with Isaiah, "Awake, awake, stand up, O Jerusalem: Loose thyself

from the bonds of thy neck, O captive daughter of Sion," but
the Fātimid leader, Iftikhār ad-Daulah, had other plans for the
weary band of crusaders. Wells outside the Holy City had been
poisoned, cattle had been driven out of reach of the invaders, and
the Christian population of the town had been sent away, lest
treason should work as it had in Antioch.

Unfavorable terrain as well as limited numbers caused the
chieftains to decide to undertake only a partial investment of
Jerusalem. Robert of Normandy and Robert of Flanders besieged
the walls from the north, while Godfrey, Tancred, and Gaston
of Béarn pitched their tents to the west. In the first of the operations Raymond occupied the area from the camp of Godfrey to
the foot of Mount Sion, but, because of a gully which prevented
close approach to the walls, he moved his tent to Mount Sion.
His chaplain pretends that his disgruntled retainers refused to
follow him until they received substantial sums to guard his
camp.

On June 9, Raymond Pilet and Raymond of Turenne made
a successful raid in which they defeated two hundred of the
enemy, while killing a few and seizing thirty horses. On the second day of the following week the early successes of the Christians emboldened them to make a frontal attack on the walls,
despite their limited number of siege ladders and machines. The
sources are rather reluctant to give a full account of their losses,
and are content to inform us that one ladder was placed against
an inner wall and that hand-to-hand fighting took place. Raymond d'Aguilers, never reluctant to emphasize the supernatural,
relates that a hermit on the Mount of Olives incited them to attack the city.[12]

As usual, the Christians learned that faith without works failed
to wrest strongholds from the Saracens. After their disappointment over the failure of the miracle promised by the hermit, new
troubles arose. The knights began to forage near and far for
food and booty, perhaps to their loss of interest in siege operations. Water became scarce and certainly most unpalatable after
being carried several miles through the summer heat in leather
containers. The pool of Siloam became contaminated, and the
ever watchful enemy lay in wait and killed the unwary. The

stench of dead animals added to the difficulties of the besiegers. But fortune always smiled on the Christians of the First Crusade, and news of the arrival on June 17 of six ships in the deserted harbor of Jaffa revived their flagging spirits.

When news of the docking of the Genoese fleet arrived in the camp, Raymond of Saint-Gilles dispatched two forces to Jaffa. One group, under Geldemar Carpinel, was composed of twenty knights and fifty horsemen, while another group of fifty knights under Raymond Pilet and William of Sabran was to follow in their wake. As the forces under Carpinel crossed the plains near Ramla, they were attacked by superior forces of the enemy. The shower of arrows felled all of the Christian bowmen as well as a few knights among whom was Achard of Montmerle. Fortunately, the forces of Pilet and William of Sabran arrived upon the scene to save the embattled Christians. The Turkish flight enabled Provençals to continue unmolested to Jaffa, where they were entertained by the Genoese sailors with a feast of bread, wine, and fish. In the festivities which followed, the sailors failed to post lookouts, and so on the following morning they learned that they had been surrounded by an enemy fleet. One of the ships managed by the use of oars and sails to break the blockade and escape to Latakia. Other sailors abandoned their ships and returned under escort to the crusading tents. The addition of Genoese workmen along with their leader, William Embriacus, improved the hopes of the besiegers. Furthermore, it seems that many crusaders who had bathed in the Jordan had hoped to sail home on the Genoese ships. With their hope of escape cut off, they were now forced to rejoin the crusading army.

During this time, perhaps in the first part of July, chieftains held a council which considered the question of Tancred's occupation of Bethlehem. Although Jerusalem remained in the hands of the enemy, the council discussed the election of a king of the city. Raymond d'Aguilers, the only eyewitness to report the meeting, states that many considered that it was not proper to have a king where the Lord was crowned. In this he reflects the feeling of the church party, which in this case was able to delay the selection of a ruler until eight days after the capture of Jerusalem. Albert of Aachen wrote that Raymond and Tancred quarreled at this time, but no witness mentions the fact, although we might well guess that the old count opposed the high-handed tactics of the Norman in the matter of Bethlehem.[13]

As usual, the siege followed two courses, one the activities of the visionaries, the other the work of the military-minded. Raymond d'Aguilers reports that Peter Desiderius, a priest who now occupied the role of the late Peter Bartholomew, had a vision in which Adhémar appeared with instructions for the people to cease their work and to go around the city barefooted. Two Provençals, Isoard of Die and William Hugh of Monteil, conveyed the celestial message to the leaders and the people, who decreed that a day be set apart for a religious procession. On July 8, a strange spectacle greeted the defenders of Jerusalem. Leading the procession of Christians came the clergy, with crosses and relics of saints, closely followed by knights and all able-bodied men, barefooted, with trumpets sounding and standards flying. At the Mount of Olives the old warriors laid aside their personal grievances and united as Christian brothers in the common cause, or at least so Raymond d'Aguilers would have us believe. Then they marched around the city, as the Fātimids jeered and desecrated the many crosses which they displayed from the walls. We wonder why they did not attack the barefooted Christians as they marched gingerly across the rough terrain.

On the other hand, realists began to prepare siege weapons as well as rolling towers. The Count of Toulouse entrusted construction work to the Genoese under the direction of William Embriacus, and assigned to the bishop of Albara the job of supervising the labor of captive Saracens. The Provençals had taken many towns and so had practically enslaved the native population. Throughout the camp it was customary to pay artisans from a common fund, except in the case of the Provençal army. Raymond paid his workmen from his own treasury. One from the entourage of the Midi, Gaston of Béarn, likewise assisted Godfrey and the two Roberts in the construction of machines and weapons. The whole operation was a stupendous task of transporting scarce materials over long distances under adverse conditions. Finally, in a surprise move on the night of July

9–10, Godfrey had a large siege tower moved to an area between the church of St. Stephen and the valley of Jehoshaphat. In the meantime, Raymond of Saint-Gilles, anxious to bring his siege tower against the wall, offered a denarius for every three stones which his men threw into a ditch which lay between Mount Sion and the south wall of Jerusalem. The task took three days, at the end of which Provençals undertook to bridge the walls. The desperate defenders hurled flaming wood dipped in pitch, wax, and sulphur. The chaplain could not refrain from reporting that two women tried to bewitch the Christians, only to meet death.

The general attack of July 13 and 14 is poorly reported by witnesses, although they are agreed upon the stubborn resistance of the defenders. At one time the assault was almost abandoned, but for some strange reason one of the knights in the service of Godfrey managed to climb over the walls from the duke's siege tower and thus lead the way to the inner city. Raymond and his men were still attacking Jerusalem to the south when news came of the success of their comrades in arms. Quick to take advantage of the panic, Provençals entered the Holy City by way of the Gate of the Tower of David. There then ensued a terrible massacre of Moslems. Raymond d'Aguilers, always at his best in describing bloody encounters, relates that wonderful scenes were enacted. Christians decapitated some, tortured others by casting them into fire, and pillaged the city at will. It was a day which marked the "justification of Christianity, the humiliation of paganism, and the renewal of faith," at least so it seemed to the count's chaplain. So elated was he over the bloody sight that for him the vision of the Apostle John was fulfilled and men rode in blood up to the bridles of their horses.[14]

The Count of Toulouse seized the Tower of David after he had promised its defenders safe conduct from Jerusalem. Again Albert of Aachen has charged Raymond with venality, saying that he received money from Iftikhār ad-Daulah, commander of the town. This is the same stock criticism of the count's greed which Albert makes consistently in his work. The author of the *Gesta* is content to state that the commander of the Tower of David opened the gate, at which pilgrims had paid tribute in the past, only after Godfrey had broken into Jerusalem. Raymond, who had besieged the gate, furnished Iftikhār ad-Daulah safe conduct to Ascalon.

Soon after the fall of the city, joyful churchmen celebrated the restoration of the Christian faith there with appropriate religious ceremonies. It is noteworthy that Greek Christian inhabitants in Jerusalem greeted the Westerners with joy, showed them sacred places, and in turn worshipped with them. The stench of the dead and the smoldering haze of the funereal fires still hung over the Holy Sepulcher when discord arose among the Christians. The delayed decision over who should be ruler now confronted the crusaders. In addition, Symeon II, the Greek patriarch, who had fled from the Fātimids, died on the island of Cyprus, leaving vacant his office, which the Christians decided to fill with a Latin. In a council held on July 22, the churchmen argued that inasmuch as spiritual affairs preceded temporal ones, so should the election of a patriarch be held before that of the ruler of Jerusalem. Despite the confused account of Raymond d'Aguilers, some believe the bishop of Albara, a close associate of Raymond of Saint-Gilles, led an unsuccessful flight to have a patriarch named at this time. Such a belief has led to the assumption that Provençals wished to push the candidacy of Raymond by first selecting a patriarch who would be in accord with the election of the count. Yet we are by no means sure that the bishop of Albara pushed the nomination of the old count. Certainly, his later actions pose the question of his support of the Count of Toulouse.

With the failure of the church party, the council then turned to the selection of a temporal ruler. Both Raymond d'Aguilers and Albert of Aachen state that the Count of Toulouse was offered the kingship of Jerusalem but that he refused. Despite many ingenious theories of secondary writers, the riddle remains unsolved. The chaplain's word in the matter has become suspect because of Raymond's subsequent actions, which have been interpreted as indicating that he begrudged Godfrey his city and sought to embarrass him by making it impossible for the defender of the Holy Sepulcher to control his possessions. After the election of Godfrey on July 22, 1099, Raymond retained the essentially strategic Tower of David. When Godfrey demanded the surrender of the tower, the Count of Toulouse, his biographer states, refused, saying that he wished to keep it until Easter. As the quarrel grew, the count of Normandy, the count of Flanders, and perhaps some Provençals supported Godfrey. Raymond bowed to the inevitable and surrendered the tower to the bishop of Albara in anticipation of a judgment. The bishop turned it over to Godfrey without awaiting judgment, perhaps under pressure. Unfortunately, the author of the *Gesta* gives us no information on the quarrel.

We cannot, of course, be sure that the Count of Saint-Gilles did not covet Jerusalem. On the other hand, we believe the tradition that he was offered the city probably reflects nothing more than the feeling that it was proper that the post should have been offered to him and likewise appropriate that, as a pilgrim, he should refuse it. If the count was seeking control of the city, he must have recognized that certain obstacles stood in his way. The Latin clergy had no desire to share their newly won offices with the minions of Alexius, and they must have weighed Raymond's policy of Greek friendship as more than overbalancing his former deeds of charity. In the ranks of the laymen, his Provençals were restive and anxious to return to their homelands. One suggestion is that they failed to champion the cause of their indefatigable leader and chose the lesser evil, the more pliable Godfrey. Provençals supported Godfrey both before and after the siege of Jerusalem, and without them he could not have succeeded. Gaston of Béarn, Gerard of Roussillon, Raimbaud of Orange, and William V of Montpellier were included in this group. At least two, Raimbaud and William, owed him allegiance, and the others were close associates.[15]

We can feel that, in this alignment of Provençals with Godfrey, there should be understood the tacit consent of the Count of Toulouse. It is not likely that the crusade, which was sufficiently well organized to achieve its goal, had in such a short time reached the state of anarchy where the count's vassals would move to violate the *salva fidelitate* clause by which they would qualify any service to a lord other than the Count of Toulouse. Legally, their lands and, conceivably, hostages stood for their relationship to their head. They owed him counsel, and in concert they might prevail over him and influence his policies. But they could not become openly or actively hostile to him without laying themselves open to penalties. In the light of such reasoning, it would seem that if Raymond had desired to hold the Tower of David, Godfrey could not have mustered sufficient force to oust him.

The chaplain took advantage of the incident to give the count apostolic stature. He relates that Raymond, when denied his legal rights, considered that he had been dishonored and consequently went out from the city. We seem to see him shaking the dust from his feet and refusing to remain where he had been dishonored. Yet, in denial of this incident, we find him in Jerusalem shortly thereafter, and later lending his support to the destruction of the city's Moslem foes before Ascalon. It seems possible, if the chaplain's allegory is rooted in fact, that the count, preferring to give active assignments to other men, very likely concurred in Godfrey's appointment as defender of Jerusalem, a post which may, according to the count's thinking, simply have involved protecting the interests of the church and the pilgrims in the locality. Jerusalem, the object of the holy quest, must have appeared to him as a possession of the church in which he himself, as well as other patrons, would have some rights and holdings. Godfrey's contention that he was a liege lord due homage for possessions in Jerusalem was not according to Raymond's understanding. Such is indicated by his surrendering his possessions to the jurisdiction of the church in the person of Peter of Albara. Raymond had many times returned his disputed lands and rights to the church and had been praised by popes for such acts. Now, because of a figure evoked by the chaplain, he has borne censure for his behavior in the matter of the Tower of David. That Raymond's thinking must have carried some weight is suggested by the knowledge that Provençals did remain in Jerusalem, presumably with possessions.

Despite the chaplain's report of his master's bad sportsmanship over possession of the Tower of David, Raymond accepted the *fait accompli*, left Jerusalem on July 28, and, like a good pilgrim, went to bathe in the river Jordan. Following the instructions which Peter Bartholomew had given months before, the Count of Saint-Gilles gathered palms and, along with his chaplain, crossed the river on a wickerwork raft. Clad in a fresh shirt and new breeches, he could well believe that as a true crusader he had fulfilled his crusading vows without material gain, and, like his chaplain, he could wonder why Peter Bartholomew had so instructed him. Raymond d'Aguilers reports that the Count of Saint-Gilles was still bitter over his ill treatment when he returned to Jerusalem to make preparations to leave the Holy Land. In the meantime, Arnulf, chaplain of the count of Normandy, was chosen patriarch of Jerusalem despite the bitter opposition of Raymond d'Aguilers and other churchmen. Perhaps suspicious of Raymond's intentions, and ever mindful of the appeal of the Holy Lance, the wily patriarch insisted that the natives of the Holy City unearth the true Cross. The new-found relic became the object of great reverence, and replaced the Holy Lance in the minds of many Christians who remained in Jerusalem.[16]

While Raymond tarried in Jerusalem, news came that al-Afdal Shāhānshāh, vizir of Egypt, was in Ascalon preparing an attack upon the Christians. Godfrey, Robert of Flanders, and the newly elected patriarch, Arnulf of Chocques, marched out of the city to investigate the rumor. Raymond of Saint-Gilles and Robert of Normandy remained in the city until the advanced units confirmed the report. Scholars who attempt to explain this delay of Raymond as a continuation of his personal feud with Godfrey are probably mistaken. Raymond d'Aguilers states that the leaders agreed to follow a plan of battle which first called for a reconnoitering party to determine the position and strength of the enemy as well as the need for reinforcements. He also leads us to believe that only after the princes and the priests walked with bare feet before the Sepulcher of the Lord did they decide upon defense of their newly won lands. The author of the *Gesta* does not incriminate Raymond. To him, it seemed that Raymond and the count of Normandy wanted to be certain of the rumors of the approach of al-Afdal before they moved. So it seems that if modern critics care to use this simple statement from the *Gesta* to condemn Raymond, they should also include Robert Curthose in their character assassination.

The response of the Count of Toulouse to the appeal of Godfrey leaves no room for criticism of his actions. After praying to

God for aid, the old count and his followers, strengthened by
the Holy Lance, rushed to the relief of their fellow Christians
on August 10, and on the following day joined forces with them.
By this time the crusaders were thoroughly aroused by the stories
that al-Afdal planned to slay all of the older Christians, leaving
only the younger ones to intermingle with the Fātimids and so
produce a race of warriors. It was reported that the Fātimids
planned to destroy Jerusalem as the last memorial to the Lord.
As usual, the Latins forgot their quarrels and united in the common cause. Late on August 11 the Christians, coming unexpectedly upon three hundred Saracens, routed them and seized
a large number of cattle and sheep, in addition to a few prisoners
from whom they learned that al-Afdal planned to recapture
Jerusalem.

On August 12, the crusaders prepared to engage the Fātimids
in a battle which takes its name from Ascalon, a coastal town
located west of the Holy City. The preceding night had been one
of mixed blessings for them. No tents had been pitched and their
rest was disturbed. Bread, wine, grain, and salt had been absent
from their meals, but meat was in abundance. The enemy, aroused
by trumpets and horns early in the morning, were not happy in
the choice of the site of battle. Their soothsayers and stargazers
reported that the signs were not propitious and advised, in vain,
against combat. In the line of battle Raymond of Saint-Gilles
occupied the right flank near the sea, Godfrey the left, and the
count of Normandy, the count of Flanders, Tancred, and Gaston
of Béarn took up their positions in the center. Foot soldiers and
bowmen preceded the knights into battle.

The Fātimids were prepared for desert warfare with water bags
hanging from their necks, perhaps, as the Christians thought, to
enable them to pursue their enemies for many miles. But it was
not to be the case. As Christians moved forward in orderly ranks,
al-Afdal, probably surprised by the sudden attack, attempted to
check their advance with his archers. Fortunately, the count of
Normandy spotted the vizir's standard, a golden apple on top
of a spear. Dashing wildly into the ranks of the enemy, the Norman wounded al-Afdal and set an example for his fellow warriors.
Tancred followed through with a charge into the middle of the

Fātimid battle line. As the center of the line collapsed, a rout ensued. Raymond of Saint-Gilles, the scourge of the Moslems, relentlessly pursued the enemy. Many of them threw themselves into the sea in preference to falling into the hands of the Provençals. In some quarters, the Fātimids climbed trees to escape the fury of their pursuers, only to be shot from their lofty perches by archers. Those who dared to surrender were decapitated by merciless Christians, who butchered them, in the words of the *Gesta,* as though they were animals being cut to pieces for the market. As the fighting ended, crusaders turned to the collection of spoils—gold, silver, sheep, cattle, and great quantities of food. Heaped with worldly goods, they returned joyfully to Jerusalem.[17]

Events which followed the battle of Ascalon, August 13–17, have been reconstructed largely from the account of Baldric of Dol, Albert of Aachen, and Ralph of Caen, none of whom were there. Supposedly, inhabitants of Ascalon, aware of the protection which Raymond had given to Saracens in the Tower of David, now threw themselves upon his mercy. In response to their entreaties, he dispatched a small force from Jerusalem to accept the offer of the Ascalonites and to give them a banner to fly from their walls. Later, when Godfrey and Raymond arrived outside the walls of Ascalon, they quarreled so violently over the possession of the town that the residents refused to surrender. It is quite possible that originally Raymond had sent a renegade Turk, Bohémond, to treat with al-Afdal with a view to learning the plans of the Fātimids. However, in his usual anti-Provençal vein, Albert of Aachen accuses Raymond of advising the enemy to defend themselves against Godfrey. The Oriental sources, which are probably more accurate in this case, indicate that the Ascalonites had to purchase immunity for their city, but that a quarrel among the crusading chiefs saved them from paying tribute.

So it seems that Raymond, finding that Godfrey blocked his efforts to secure money from the defenders, withdrew from the contest, thereby leaving Godfrey too weak to carry on without his aid. It is quite unlikely that Raymond, as many writers believe, ever aspired to make a serious bid for possession of Ascalon. Tactics suggested some action pursuant to the conquest of the

Fātimids, but Godfrey's jealousy made concerted action impossible and thus forfeited the fruits of victory. Albert, in defense of his hero, Godfrey, was apparently anxious to blame his failure to seize Ascalon upon the Count of Saint-Gilles, rather than to explain that the other leaders, having fulfilled their crusading vows, were no more anxious than Raymond to engage in a siege which would delay their departure from Palestine. United effort to recover the Holy Sepulcher was one thing; a siege of Ascalon was quite another problem. The war was over and the weary participants were ready to return to their homes. Later, historians had to find a scapegoat for the shortcomings of the people, and without compunction they turned to Raymond.

Leaving Godfrey in front of the walls of Ascalon, the crusading princes took the coastal route to Arsuf. Hoping that the inhabitants would surrender, Raymond remained near the town for a day and a night. Albert of Aachen again accuses Raymond of perfidy when he relates that the Count of Toulouse, upon learning that Godfrey approached Arsuf, advised the inhabitants to hold out and then rejoined Robert of Flanders and Robert of Normandy, who were encamped near Caesarea. Albert further relates that when Godfrey learned of this trick of Raymond, only the intervention of the crusading leaders prevented him from attacking the old count. However, the discord suddenly ceased, and harmony again prevailed in the camp of the Christians. We know that Godfrey later failed to capture Arsuf, and it is quite probable that Albert, who may have accepted Norman propaganda, gladly blamed the mistakes of Godfrey upon the unpopular Raymond.

In reviewing the events of the fall of Jerusalem and the aftermath—the possession of the Tower of David and the quarrel of Raymond and Godfrey at Ascalon and Arsuf—many scholars have falsely concluded that Raymond was guilty of poor sportsmanship. Yet, when Norman propaganda has been deleted, there seems to be little information left upon which to base a charge of perfidy against Raymond. Albert's accusations against the count reflect his efforts to cover up the failures of Godfrey. Raymond d'Aguilers' remarks can scarcely be accounted more than a literary excursion. Perhaps the best reply to the count's critics is the question, could any of the crusading princes have assembled the Christians in January of 1099 before the crumbled walls of Ma'arrat-an-Nu'mān and led them more rapidly and successfully to Jerusalem? From the standpoint of supplies, military problems, and Turkish opposition, the question seems to call for a negative reply.[18]

NOTES

1. Raymond d'Aguilers, *op. cit.*, p. 272; *Gesta*, p. 180; C. W. David, *Robert Curthose*, pp. 109–10; Nicholson, *op. cit.*, p. 76; W. B. Stevenson, *The Crusaders in the East*, p. 31. Critics, overlooking military needs, mistakenly assume that the slowness of the march indicates Raymond's desire to regain his lost power in Antioch.

2. Raymond d'Aguilers, *op. cit.*, p. 273; *Gesta*, p. 182.

3. Raymond d'Aguilers, *op. cit.*, p. 273; *Gesta*, p. 182; Dussaud, *op. cit.*, p. 92; E. G. Rey, *Les colonies franques de Syrie aux XII*e *et XIII*e *siècles*, p. 126; Paul Deschamps, *Les châteaux des croisés en Terre Sainte*, pp. 113–15.

4. Raymond d'Aguilers, *op. cit.*, pp. 274–75; *Gesta*, p. 184; Heinrich von Sybel, *op. cit.*, p. 392.

5. Raymond d'Aguilers, *op. cit.*, pp. 275–76; *Gesta*, pp. 188–90; Dussaud, *op. cit.*, pp. 85, 94; *Kreuzzugsbriefe*, p. 170. See footnote 56. Hill, *op. cit.*, *Speculum*, p. 275.

6. Raymond d'Aguilers, *op. cit.*, pp. 276–78; *Gesta*, pp. 184–88; Albert of Aachen, *op. cit.*, pp. 453–55; Riant, *op. cit.*, I, 189; Ibn al-Athīr, *op. cit.*, pp. 204–205.

7. Raymond d'Aguilers, *op. cit.*, pp. 278, 286; *Gesta*, p. 186; Nicholson, *op. cit.*, p. 82; M. M. Knappen, "Robert II of Flanders in the First Crusade," in *Munro Essays*, pp. 91–98; Grousset, *op. cit.*, p. 134, note 5; Riant, *op. cit.*, I, p. 192; Chalandon, *op. cit.* ("Essai"), pp. 214–16.

8. Raymond d'Aguilers, *op. cit.*, p. 277; *Gesta*, pp. 188–90, and note 1, p. 190; Karl Baedeker, *Palestine et Syrie*, pp. 1, liii. The harvest in the region under discussion started in April and May. Wheat and barley probably supplied the crusaders, and harvesting probably determined in part their plans.

9. Raymond d'Aguilers, *op. cit.*, pp. 279–80; Maury, *op. cit.*, pp. 401–

403; Benjamin Thorpe, *The Homilies of the Anglo-Saxon Church,* II, 339. In efforts to explain, some have attempted to show that Peter became a tool of the Count of Toulouse. They overlook the fact that the canon of Le Puy is not reporting as an historian but is using the episode to display his knowledge. His conception of the Lord fits into iconographic patterns of the eleventh century. He also reveals his slavish adherence to biographical patterns by his frequent use of ranks and gradations of sinners.

10. Raymond d'Aguilers, *op. cit.,* pp. 280–90; Ralph of Caen, *op. cit.,* p. 682; H. C. Lea, *Superstition and Force,* pp. 305–306; The pattern of this ordeal is typical of many others. The elaborate details of the piles of wood, the victim emerging from the fire unhurt, and the wild mob later crushing him are current devices of storytellers. Howorth remarks that when the fictitious is told as the truth it is often a literary device rather than the mark of an uncritical mind. See Henry H. Howorth, *Saint Gregory the Great,* pp. 237–38; Paulin Paris, *op. cit.,* I, xxi. Paris looked upon the canon of Le Puy as a fraud; Guibert of Nogent, *op. cit.,* p. 252.

11. Raymond d'Aguilers, *op. cit.,* pp. 288–92; *Gesta,* pp. 190–94; William of Tyre, *op. cit.,* p. 311.

12. Fulcher, *op. cit.,* p. 354; Raymond d'Aguilers, *op. cit.,* pp. 293–94; *Gesta,* pp. 194–98; William of Tyre, *op. cit.,* p. 318.

13. Raymond d'Aguilers, *op. cit.,* pp. 294–96; *Gesta,* pp. 198–202; Albert of Aachen, *op. cit.,* pp. 482–83; Nicholson, *op. cit.,* p. 90.

14. Raymond d'Aguilers, *op. cit.,* pp. 296–300; *Gesta,* pp. 202–206; Ibn al-Athīr, *op. cit.,* p. 198; *Apocalypsis B. Joannis Apostoli,* XIV:20.

15. Raymond d'Aguilers, *op. cit.,* pp. 300–301; *Gesta,* p. 206; Albert of Aachen, *op. cit.,* pp. 483–89; A. C. Krey, ed. and tr., *A History of Deeds Done Beyond the Sea,* I, 380, note 1; Grousset, *op. cit.,* p. 317; *Kamāl-ad-Dīn, op. cit.,* pp. 587–88; Abou'l Fedâ, pp. 3–4; Stevenson, *op. cit.,* p. 36; David, *op. cit.,* pp. 119–21, 189–200. The fact that other leaders were refused the honor emphasizes the idea that the title carried little more than that of protector of the church. In the paucity of sources we can only conjecture concerning the truth of the canon's report. Some scholars do not agree with the idea that Godfrey's power was limited by the church. See John Gordon Rowe, "Paschal II and the Latin Orient," in *Speculum,* XXXII (July, 1957); John Gordon Rowe, "The Papacy and the Greeks (1122–1153)," in *Church History,* XXVIII (September, 1959).

16. Raymond d'Aguilers, *op. cit.,* 301; Jean Richard, *Le royaume latin de Jérusalem,* p. 32; Jean Richard, *Le Comté de Tripoli sous la dynastie toulousaine* (1102–1187), pp. 9–10. We prefer to follow the continuation of *Historia Francorum qui ceperunt Jerusalem,* in which the

author states, "Hisque peractis, reversi sumus Jerosolymam," which indicates that Raymond returned to Jerusalem. Runciman believes that Raymond remained in Jericho because of his quarrel with Godfrey; Matthew 11:11–17; Mark 6:10–11; Luke 9:4–5.

17. *Gesta*, pp. 208–16; Raymond d'Aguilers, *op. cit.*, pp. 302–305; Otto Heerman, *Die Gefechtsführung der abendländischen Heere im Orient in der Epoche des ersten Kreuzzuges*, pp. 49–58; Hans Delbrück, *Geschichte der kriegskunst in Rahmen der politischen Geschichte*, pp. 418–19; Matthew of Edessa, *Extraits de la chronique de Matthieu d'Edesse*, in *RHC Arm.* I, 46; Ibn al-Athīr, *op. cit.*, p. 202. A renegade Moslem wrote: "Avec ton épée tu as fait triompher la religion du Messie; honneur à toi, Saint-Gilles! Jamais les hommes n'ont entendu parler d'une déroute plus honteuse que cell d'El-Afdal."

18. Baldricus, *op. cit.*, p. 111; Albert of Aachen, *op. cit.*, pp. 497–98; Ralph of Caen, *op. cit.*, p. 703; Ibn al-Athīr, *op. cit.*, p. 202; Ibn al-Qalānisī, *The Damascus Chronicle of the Crusades*, p. 49.

VII

COMPLETION OF A VOW

RAYMOND OF SAINT-GILLES had taken a vow never to return to his native land, at least so the chroniclers would have us believe. Now, with the Holy Sepulcher recovered, he found himself without a domain. Baldwin, Bohémond, and even Godfrey had profited from the desertion of their native lands, and only Raymond remained a crusader without a county, principality, or a kingdom. Although the church promised followers of the Cross rewards both here and in the hereafter if they performed their vows, the comrades of Raymond and even moderns seemed to begrudge the old Count of Toulouse any possessions in the Levant. Yet we know that the success of the whole crusading venture lay in the conquest of the Moslem seaboard and in the rapid colonization of it.

As Raymond in the company of the two Roberts left Caesarea and journeyed to Latakia, there were several courses of action which he could take. Betrayed by Bohémond and rebuffed by the jealous defender of the Holy Sepulcher, Raymond could have returned to the Midi without disgrace, because he had performed his vow to retake the Holy City. For a man of his advanced years such a course of action seemed logical, but he would not take it. If refusing to return home suggests a former vow to forsake his native land, then it follows that from the beginning he had planned to assist in making permanent the Christian hold on the Moslem lands. His critics, confused by Norman propaganda, have urged that he cast his eyes toward Antioch and hoped to aid Alexius in ousting Bohémond. But again this is conjecture. Later actions of Raymond strengthen our belief that as he journeyed to Latakia, he had hopes of forming the county of Tripoli as a refuge for pilgrims and a foothold against the Moslems, but such desires need not have been concomitant to war upon the Norman prince.

Events of the past support the idea that Raymond was never interested in the emperor's lands beyond the limits of the oath which he had made to him. In all of his efforts the Count of Toulouse had been careful to return lands which belonged to Alexius. In contrast, in Saracen lands he sought to establish some form of suzerainty. That Raymond respected his oath to the basileus and returned to him his ancient towns is corroborated by Anna. But, as early as the summer of 1098, the Provençal leader had shown an interest in areas south of Antioch and had gained claims to Tel-Mannas, Albara, Ma'arrat-an-Nu'mān, Arzghān, Belmesyn (perhaps Melmeshan), and Rugia, which moderns locate as Chastel-Rouge. That he seriously considered establishing a state this far north in 1098 may be considered doubtful. Leaving Albara and Ma'arrat-an-Nu'mān, the count had continued his journey to Jerusalem, and only the fact that the successors of Peter of Albara remained on good terms with Raymond's descendants would lead us to believe that he dreamed of a Syrian state in this area.

Only when Raymond turned south on his journey to recover the Holy Sepulcher do we see some pattern for a future county of Tripoli. Perhaps as early as the siege of Antioch, Raymond had knowledge of Tripoli, both through Christian emissaries who had visited with the Fātimids and through his Genoese allies. Raymond d'Aguilers relates that a priest, Everard, had been in Tripoli at the time of the siege of Antioch. Certainly, as the crusaders marched toward the Holy City, Raymond conquered or established his suzerainty in Kafartāb, Rafanīyah, Hisn al-Akrād, Tortosa, and Maraclea. But one area, 'Arqah, the key to Tripoli, had attracted him and brought him criticism despite his abandonment of its siege. Apparently Raymond believed that Tripoli was without a substantial Greek claim; for his later interests point to a determined effort to carve a county in its environs. So, as Raymond journeyed northward in 1099, the peaceful Ibn-'Ammār might well have understood that days of trouble lay ahead for the emirate of Tripoli.

But whatever dreams Raymond may have entertained, we are certain that he had little time to forget the old difficulties with his Norman rival. Arriving at Jabala in September, 1099, he found Bohémond attempting to take Latakia from the Byzantines who had occupied it. How the imperial forces had gained it remains one of the riddles of the First Crusade; but in line with Raymond's consistent Greek rapprochement, it appears that he surrendered the town to Alexius on the eve of his departure for Jerusalem, after having taken possession of it as early as 1098 upon the cession of it to him by either Guynemer the Pirate or Edgar Atheling. To complicate matters, Daimbert, the archbishop of Pisa, was assisting in the blockade of the city. Raymond, true to form, challenged Bohémond and threatened to attack him. For the first time, Raymond received the full support of his comrades-in-arms. Daimbert, unable to justify his participation in this attack on fellow Christians, apologized and withdrew from the siege. Bohémond, deprived of moral support, gave up and permitted Raymond to enter Latakia. The old count then placed his banner over the city, and installed a garrison of five hundred Provençals. Latakia now became a base for future Provençal operations, a thorn in the expansionist hopes of the Normans, and a base for Greek-Provençal bargaining. According to Albert of Aachen, Raymond was again abiding by his oath to Alexius in upholding Greek rights to Latakia.[1]

If the Count of Saint-Gilles' action is so simply explained by Albert, the reversal of Daimbert's stand and the unusual spirit of cooperation of the two Roberts pose a more difficult problem. It is quite true that Daimbert had been with Urban during his trip to southern France, and he may well have been acquainted with his crusading plans, in addition to having an understanding that the Count of Toulouse was on good terms with the pope. So it is possible that he respected the advice of Raymond in his insistence on Greek and Latin friendship. Again it must be borne in mind that, as a politician, he sensed the danger of continued quarreling between the Count of Saint-Gilles and Bohémond and, as an intermediary, he may have hoped to compromise their differences. The action of Robert of Normandy and Robert of Flanders is partly explainable in the fact that they now needed to regain their homeland, and the emperor could help them to receive passage to the West. It would be only wise for them to support the cause of his best Latin friend as well as to uphold the claims of the basileus to Latakia. To give them the benefit of some honorable feeling, it may likewise be true that they had become disgusted with the pettiness of Godfrey and the newly revealed cupidity of Bohémond, and that they expressed a genuine respect for Raymond, to say nothing of their desire to leave the Levant as friends of a man who, more nearly than any other, had led the Christians to the Holy Sepulcher.[2]

Raymond decided to remain at Latakia while his comrades, Robert of Flanders, Robert of Normandy, and Gaston of Béarn, sailed for home by way of Constantinople. The obscurity of his movements, between September of 1099 and May or June of 1100, has caused critics of Raymond to assume that he made plans to continue the Norman feud. Fulcher intimates that at this time Raymond jealously guarded Latakia and Tortosa from the Normans, and modern historians, in writing history backwards, have assumed that he dreamed of combining his forces with those of Alexius to regain Antioch. We are further confused by a letter of Daimbert in which he states that Raymond promised to go to Jerusalem again. If such a promise were made, it would lead to the conclusion that the old count planned, at this early time, to lead another group of crusaders across Anatolia and retrace the journey to the Holy Sepulcher, but again these speculations have very little to support them.

Certain bits of evidence lead more strongly to the conclusion that Raymond was pointing, in 1099, to the creation of the county of Tripoli. If he did promise Daimbert to return to Jerusalem, it would be more to the point that he planned to use reinforcements from the West to strengthen the poorly manned strongholds of Christendom, rather than to lead the so-called Crusade of 1101 against Antioch, as moderns have assumed. But in 1099 recruits were far away from the Levant, and the most tangible plan would have called for the investment of Tripoli. From a long-range view, Raymond no doubt hoped to take the hinterland and starve the Tripolitans to surrender.

Most tangible evidence that Raymond aspired to carve a new state in Tripoli comes from the pens of Anna and Ralph. They state that he attacked the area at this time. Chalandon and Röhricht support their statements. Of course, due to the small number of Provençals willing to remain in the Near East, Raymond's efforts must have been largely confined to raids. William of Tyre gives further strength to the count's plan to seize Tripoli by stating that he went to the court of Alexius to receive aid for the seizure of the new state from the Moslems. His statement seems to be a clear and concise summary of the motivating force behind Raymond's continued stay in the Levant.

Intangible, but yet very provocative, is a statement that Daimbert remained in the neighborhood of Raymond's dominion at Latakia and Valania for several months. One must not forget that Daimbert had been on excellent terms with Alfonso, and one may well assume that Elvira was anxious for news from Spain. Furthermore, Daimbert brought Bohémond and Raymond face to face after the quarrel at Latakia. Supposedly, concord reigned between the two. It is possible that there was an understanding at this time that Raymond could carve a new state from Tripoli without Norman intervention. Events of later years strongly suggest it.

Several reports have stood in the way of the acceptance of a theory that Raymond and Bohémond worked out a *modus vivendi*. Fulcher relates that when Bohémond made a delayed pilgrimage to the Holy Sepulcher, Baldwin was able to receive ample supplies in Latakia on his way to rendezvous with the Norman leader at Valania. However, on the return journey, supplies were not sold to the returning pilgrims because of a scarcity of goods in Latakia. Moderns have assumed that the old count took this chance for revenge upon Bohémond. But Fulcher did not state such a fact and even takes pains to write that he regretted that Raymond could not accompany the pilgrims to Jerusalem. A second event likewise is used to implicate Raymond. After the death of Godfrey in July of 1100, Morellus, secretary of Daimbert, was sent by his master and Tancred to inform Bohémond of the fact. Albert, far removed from the scene and often in error, reported falsely that Raymond seized Morellus, thereby preventing Bohémond from receiving the news. So moderns have thus concluded that the old count withheld the crown of Jerusalem from his former rival. Yet we know that Raymond had already sailed for Constantinople. So we prefer to believe, along with Anna, Ralph of Caen, William of Tyre, Röhricht, and Chalandon, that as early as 1099 or 1100 Raymond made certain thrusts against Tripoli which indicated his interest in forming a new county there, rather than to agree with the idea that he sought to continue an impractical feud with Bohémond and unite with Alexius to regain the latter's princely city of Antioch.[3]

In May or June of 1100, Raymond set sail for Constantinople with plans for working out a compact with Alexius by which he could gain aid and legal recognition for a conquest of Tripoli. It was probably understood that he would surrender Latakia, Maraclea, and Valania to the emperor. Although Ordericus Vitalis tells us that Raymond's wife gave birth to a son at Constantinople, it is probable that he left Elvira and a Provençal garrison in Latakia to await his return. During his absence the Provençals fared badly, failing to take Jabala and also losing Tortosa. Carrying the Holy Lance with him, the Count of Toulouse sailed to Cyprus and thence to Constantinople, where Alexius greeted him in August. Anna would lead us to believe that he was again offered the crown of Jerusalem during his absence in the Greek metropolis, but her statement is suspect.

During the following months the activities of Raymond are obscure. In the early months of 1101, a new mass of crusaders began to approach Constantinople and to bring fears again to Alexius. In such a state of affairs, he turned to Raymond to aid him in handling the unruly Westerners. The archbishop of Milan and his Lombard contingents, Conrad, constable of Henry IV, and his German warriors, Stephen of Blois, and Stephen, Count of Burgundy, after the usual amenities with the emperor, encamped at Nicomedia. The Count of Toulouse, now respected by the newcomers as one of the great leaders of the First Crusade, aided in negotiations between Alexius and the Latins and was chosen to act as leader and guide. To show his good will, Alexius also furnished a Greek commander, Tsitas, and some five hundred Turcopoles. We cannot be sure that the crusaders requested Raymond as their leader, or that Alexius urged them to accept him. Judging from his past record, it appears that he was still admired by the Latins, and that he and Stephen hoped to retrace the route of the First Crusade. That Alexius agreed to such a pattern seems obvious. What is not so clear is the persistence of modern scholars in urging that the basileus and Raymond, in their sinister schemes, had hoped to wreck the Norman hold on Antioch by such a move. How they might be expected to accomplish these purported objectives with an army that would destroy itself seeking to rescue Bohémond from his Turkish captors is inexplicable. In any case, it is rather futile to impute to Alexius and Raymond motives for an action which never transpired.[4]

As the Christian army moved from Nicomedia on June 3, 1101, they ignored the admonitions of Raymond and Stephen. The Lombard contingents, largest in number, changed the direction of the crusade by urging that the crusaders direct their march to Pontus. They had only recently learned that their hero, Bohémond, was held prisoner by Malik-Ghāzī-Gümüshtigin. In vain Alexius and his Western friends had attempted to dissuade them, and now they marched in one of the most futile crusades. On June 23 they captured Ankara and returned it to the emperor as they had sworn to do. On July 2, they met their first reverse when they failed to take the town of Gangra. Now the Turks began to attack stragglers, and finally, alternating with Stephen of Burgundy, Raymond again guarded the rear. Accustomed to this hazardous task, the Count of Saint-Gilles successfully discouraged sneak attacks until he was engaged by a superior force. Forced to seek aid, the old count dispatched seven knights who hurriedly brought reinforcements from the main army, but henceforth he dared not divide his army.

The journey from Gangra to the vicinity of Amasya is poorly told, but Albert in his usual inconsistent writing accuses Raymond of leading the crusaders into the barren desert because the Turks had showered him with gifts. Albert here shows his own ignorance: he was unfamiliar both with the terrain and with the practices of local Turks attempting to buy immunity. As the crusaders descended from the mountainous regions in the first week of August, they discovered the combined armies of Malik-Ghāzī-Gümüshtigin, Ridvan, and Karaja. The Turks had learned a lesson which the soldiers of the Cross had either never learned or else had forgotten. They had buried their differences and now posed the greatest threat that any crusading army had met.

Grousset locates the site of the ensuing battle between Mersivan and Amasya. The two armies met and clashed on a small scale for several days, if we may trust Albert's account. On Monday, possibly August 5, following a quiet Sabbath, Christians prepared for a showdown. The archbishop of Milan brought forth the Holy Lance which Raymond had carried with him, but its spell had been broken. Matthew of Edessa believed that this relic was a spurious one substituted by Alexius. The battle waxed and waned in favor of the Christians until the Lombards broke and ran. With them the crusaders fled in order of their battle array until even Raymond's Turcopoles abandoned him to the enemy. Even Albert, despite his anti-Provençal theme, pictures the old count taking refuge on a rocky height, fighting Turks who may well have been yelling, "Saint-Gilles, may Allah curse him!" But the grizzled warrior was durable, and through the efforts of Stephen of Blois and Conrad he was rescued from his Moslem foes.

The events of the next few hours are poorly recorded. Albert maintains that during the night the Count of Toulouse became frightened and fled to the castle of Pulveral. This cowardice made the other chiefs so panic-stricken that they left the camp in haste to the Turks, who seized and killed the camp followers. In absolute contradiction, Anna states that the crusading leaders requested Raymond and Tsitas to aid them in reaching the nearest imperial town. Since there were no eyewitness accounts, we must be content with understanding that anti-Greek propaganda had by Albert's time influenced the pens of Western writers, who were glad to make Raymond responsible for the debacle. The Count of Toulouse, like many other Christian leaders, made good his escape, leaving behind the Holy Lance, and by way of Bafra and Sinope returned to Constantinople, where Albert pretends that he was poorly received by the emperor.[5]

The lack of eyewitnesses, and the brevity and bias of the secondary accounts of the Crusade of 1101, leave Raymond's role obscure. Many interesting speculations have been voiced by historians who have become preoccupied with events which did not occur. In general, they have conjectured that the crushing defeat made Raymond less haughty, left him without a following, and ruined the possibility of reopening Anatolia to the Byzantine influence and thereby endangered the position of Bohémond. Returning from such intriguing "ifs of history," we may be satisfied to note that Raymond, as in the First Crusade, was never able to hold the unwieldy masses together. That he objected to the foolish course of the expedition is evidenced by the pen of Albert. The very inconsistency of Albert leads us to doubt that the old count maliciously led the crusaders astray in the desert. Certainly, the trust of the Christian leaders in him during the following months is more convincing than the anti-Greek propaganda of Albert. In the matter of the loss of prestige, we may note that Raymond always acted through councils for decisions. There is no evidence that his leadership in the First Crusade took any other course, and in the Crusade of 1101 he served more as a guide than a leader. As Cate has suggested, the crusaders of 1101 lost largely because of their stupidity. One might also add that the Turks had grown wiser.[6]

When the remnants of the defeated crusaders returned to Constantinople, Alexius rewarded them with gifts and permitted them to remain in his capital for several months. Albert reports that Alexius was at first angry with Raymond; however, his anger was short-lived, and once again he became friendly with the Count of Toulouse. Moderns have assumed that Alexius was bitterly disappointed over the failure of the Crusade of 1101, but again we are confronted with insufficient evidence. Whatever may have been the case, Provençal-Greek friendship was preserved.

Raymond left Constantinople toward the end of 1101 or in January of 1102. He sailed in the company of the crusaders, and

Albert reports his presence in Antioch in March in the company of Stephen of Blois, Stephen of Burgundy, Conrad, and other leaders who had been welcomed by Tancred, who had control of the city during the absence of Bohémond. Albert states that before this time Raymond had been imprisoned by Bernard the Stranger, the ruler of Tarsus. He implies that he was captured at the port of Saint Simeon, but he informs us earlier that Bernard was the governor of Longinach (Longiniada). So we are probably correct in assuming that Raymond's ship strayed and landed in the port of Tarsus. Matthew of Edessa reports that after Bernard turned him over to Tancred, he was imprisoned in a stronghold of Sarouantavi. Doubtful though Matthew's location of Raymond's prison may be, we know that the news spread and that his comrades of the disaster of 1101, supposedly those whom he had betrayed as well as the patriarch of Antioch, Bernard, interceded in his behalf and secured his release from Tancred. Albert states that Raymond was released on grounds that "ne quicquam terrae hac ex parte civitati Acrae invaderet."

Moderns have construed Raymond's oath to mean that he would desist from any efforts to gain lands between Antioch and Acre. We may well question if this is what Tancred had in mind, because we know that his interests in Acre did not carry his claims to lands to the north. Assuredly, Tancred was wise enough to know that an oath taken under duress was not binding, and he must have realized that such an oath would have forced Raymond to retire from the Levant. What is more reasonable is that Raymond gave assurance that he would not extend his southern boundary to include Acre. Following Raymond d'Aguilers, the ruler of Acre had made an accord with the Count of Toulouse in 1099, and presumably the Provençal leader held certain rights which Tancred forced him to cede as a condition for his release. Moderns have likewise assumed that Raymond promised to abandon Latakia and so was freed from further Greek commitment, but such a conclusion is hazardous. That Raymond had either returned or planned to return Latakia, Maraclea, and Valania to the Greeks is well testified to by the sources. That he planned to use Tortosa as a base, subject to the emperor's agreement, likewise seems to be proven by later events. That he had ever engaged in armed combat against his fellow Latins in behalf of Alexius has never been proven. He often came to the defense of the Greeks in council to uphold the emperor's *de jure* rights. So when Tancred later attacked the Greek town, Latakia, and Raymond did not respond with military help for the basileus, we must not assume that he was constrained by any oath to Tancred. The concord of the Count of Toulouse and the basileus continued as always—a mutual respect and understanding of the rights of equals.[7]

Following his release from Tancred, Raymond pursued a consistent policy of laying the groundwork for a new county of Tripoli, which may or may not have been dear to him because of its similarity to the Midi, as Grousset suggests. In the company of the crusading leaders who rallied to his defense in Antioch, Raymond journeyed to Tortosa, a town once captured by the Provençals and recently recaptured by the Tripolitans under the leadership of their emir. Probably strengthened by his Provençals from Latakia and a Genoese fleet, the Count of Toulouse and his friends captured the town on February 18, 1102. Röhricht and others believed that this was a violation of his oath to Tancred, but the crusading leaders did not consider it as such, and the near contemporary historians did not report it so. Albert states that by common council Raymond was chosen to defend the town, and certainly by former custom of respect for suzerainty he deserved it. But Fulcher clouds the picture when he states that the crusaders wanted Raymond to continue the march to Jerusalem, and that when he refused they reproached him. Fulcher seems to want to have the Count of Saint-Gilles journey back and forth to Jerusalem. On at least one other occasion he expressed his sorrow that the old count did not accompany the crusaders to the Holy Sepulcher. It is singularly strange that all of the other leaders could take towns and still serve the Lord but not Raymond. It simply emphasizes the fact that church writers looked upon him as a pilgrim as well as a military man. At any rate, the argument, if there was one, ended in Raymond's staying in Tortosa, while the other crusaders went on to fulfil their vows in Jerusalem.[8]

The activities of Raymond in the last few years of his life are

poorly reported by the chroniclers; however, we do know that
Raymond now planned to take Tripoli. In a charter to the abbey
of Sainte-Marie-Latine, the Count of Toulouse conveyed this information by stating that at Tortosa he had made a promise
to Peter Olivar to give him a church at Tripoli. So Raymond
devoted his efforts to forming a new state, but the steps by which
he undertook it are confusing. Fakhr al-Mulk was not slow to
meet the challenge of his old enemy who had reappeared to contest his control of Tripoli. Janāh ad-Daulah, atabeg of Homs,
sent Yakhaz with a force, while Dukak of Damascus sent two
thousand knights from his city to bolster the defense of the
Tripolitans. Without an eyewitness to help us, the secondary
account of Ibn al-Athīr is unsatisfactory. Certainly, the ensuing
events are confused.

Raymond seems to have had a force of three hundred knights.
We are told that one hundred fought the Tripolitans, another
hundred met the relief army from Damascus, and fifty others
held those from Homs, while fifty stood as reserves. In the course
of the battle the men of Homs fled and turned the battle into
a rout. The fantastic feats of the Provençals tax our credulity.
Anna comes to our aid by maintaining that the battle was fought
in Tortosa and was won by a clever ruse of the Count of Toulouse, who had withdrawn from the city unexpectedly and attacked the unwary Turks. Despite the Turkish debacle, Tripoli
was too strong for Raymond to attack, and Fakhr al-Mulk paid
sufficient tribute to check Raymond. Although at least one Moslem writer has stated that shortly before the death of Raymond
the emir of Tripoli had given him permission to control the
faubourg of the town, it is quite possible that he may have confused the time with the agreement of the two in 1102.[9]

Whatever may have happened following his successes against
the Turks, two undertakings overshadowed the activities of Raymond—the attempted conquest of al-Buqai‘ah and the building
of Mount Pilgrim. The dates of the projects are uncertain. In
turning to conquer the frontier lands of Janāh-ad-Daulah, Raymond could isolate Tripoli, and so, no doubt, work on the two
projects at the same time. It is likely that in the spring of 1102
(although some believe 1103) the old warrior moved toward

Rafanīyah, possible key to Tripoli, and then turned to attack
Tuban, a fortress located between Tortosa and Homs. In the
unsuccessful attack on Tuban, one of Raymond's warriors was
captured and held without ransom. In vain the Provençal leader
offered ten thousand pieces of gold or one thousand prisoners.
Undismayed by this ill fortune, Raymond turned to besiege
Hisn al-Akrād, a fortification which the Provençals had captured
on their way to Jerusalem in 1099, but had later abandoned to
the Turks. During the course of the siege, word came to Raymond
that his enemy Janāh ad-Daulah had been assassinated by political enemies as he was making his way from the mosque of Homs
after offering prayers for victory over Sanjiles. Quickly abandoning the siege of Hisn al-Akrād, the old count rushed to besiege
Homs but upon arriving there found that Dukak of Damascus
was marching to aid the town. Unable to meet a superior force
of Turks, Raymond exacted a tax from the inhabitants of Homs
and abandoned the siege on May 14, 1102.

The other project, the building of Mount Pilgrim, poses the
problem of determining the date of the beginning of the structure. Anna and Ralph lead us to believe that it was started before
Raymond went to Constantinople, while Albert informs us that
it was undertaken two years before the death of Raymond. However, it seems that neither 1100 nor 1103 is a correct date. It is
possible that he started the construction of Mount Pilgrim in
1102, after his success against the Tripolitans. No doubt the
building took many months, in the course of which Alexius
instructed the duke of Cyprus, Eumathius, to send needed masons
and materials. The fleets of the Genoese and Pisans also assisted
in the work. We cannot agree with some that Alexius aided in
this structure because of Raymond's assistance in his defense of
Latakia, 1102–1103, against Tancred. The poorly reported action makes any contribution of Raymond to the cause of Alexius
in this instance doubtful. The most convincing bit of evidence
that Mount Pilgrim had been started in 1102 comes from Raymond in his grant to the abbey of Sainte-Marie-Latine in 1103
in which he styles himself Count of Toulouse and Count of
Tripoli and writes of being in the suburb, in Mount Pilgrim,
a newly built castle (*noviter edificati castri*). Moreover, some

Western writers believed that Alphonse-Jourdain was born in the newly erected castle in 1103 and baptized in the Jordan. But Ordericus Vitalis writes that he was born in Constantinople, and we believe that Jourdain was a family name rather than one drawn from the Jordan River.[10]

Whatever may be the truth concerning the date of the beginning of the building of Mount Pilgrim, we are sure that it was completed in 1103, and that it was intended to be a haven for pilgrims as well as a threat to the Moslems. The year, 1103, marks several pious acts of Raymond both in behalf of Western abbeys or churches as well as Eastern ones. Richard has noted that piety marked these acts in most cases rather than his desire for revenue. The Eastern churches, oppressed for years by the Moslems, were in no position to make the grants profitable. On January 17, 1103, the Count of Saint-Gilles made a donation to the abbey of Saint-Victor of Marseilles. This grant of one half the town of Jubail was made before the conquest of the Moslem possession. Some historians think that, following his unsuccessful attack on Homs, Raymond turned to attack Tripoli and, failing there, enlisted the aid of the Genoese and Pisans to attack Jubail. However, other historians believe that Jubail fell on April 28, 1104, and the Moslems reported that the Christians tortured the natives to find the hiding places of their gold. It was likewise at this time that a Moslem historian wrote that Raymond assisted Baldwin in an attack on Acre. If this is true, it seems that the Count of Toulouse was again coming to the aid of the kingdom of Jerusalem, as he had done in the battle of Ascalon. We may be content with noting that Jubail became a part of the county of Tripoli, and Raymond had anticipated its capture in his grant to Saint-Victor of Marseilles.

Richard believes that Raymond of Saint-Gilles also gave to Saint-Ruf of Valence the church of Artucia (Orthosias) with the promise of a church in Tripoli. To Eastern churches or abbeys the Count of Toulouse was, as Richard points out, favorable to those venerated by pilgrims or ones destined to assist pilgrims in fulfilling their vows. It is probable that the Hospital de Saint-Jean, the Holy Sepulcher, Sainte-Marie-Latine, Mont Thabor, and the chapter of Bethlehem were recipients of grants from Raymond. Included in these were churches and lands in the environs of Tripoli.

As Raymond strengthened his hold on Mount Pilgrim and the neighboring towns, recruits from the Midi came to join his cause. By 1103 we know that both veterans and newcomers were in his camp. Bernard-Aton, viscount of Béziers, Aycard of Marseilles, Bérengar of Narbonne, Richard, abbot of Saint-Victor of Marseilles, the bishop of Glandève, William Hugo, William Arvei (probably of Nîmes), Ribod, Raymond of Cornelio, Bertrand Arvei, William Ariols, Pons of Fos, and William Peyre by their signatures reveal their presence at Mount Pilgrim. It is also likely that Raymond received help from the Maronite Christians, who were glad to assist in overthrowing the Moslems.[11]

Conflicting reports of the last few months of Raymond's life beset us. Moslem writers relate that, in a Tripolitan raid on Mount Pilgrim, Raymond was trapped in the flaming timbers of a house and died there as a result of injuries received. Western sources do not indicate that his death resulted from such injuries, but some moderns have pieced the story together and have concluded that he was injured in the autumn of 1104 and lingered for several months. However, Ibn al-Athīr states that the Count of Saint-Gilles survived the attack only ten days. It was a fitting end for Sanjil to die at the hands of the enemy, at least so a Moslem would have preferred to write it, and so would we prefer to see him leave the world as a doughty old warrior, fighting a good fight, and dying with his armor on and his sword flashing. But the Western sources do not help us, and we may conclude that the ravages of time, rather than the blows of the Moslems, brought the "most excellent leader of the Christian militia" to the fulfilment of his vow to recover the Holy Sepulcher and never return to his native land.

In a codicil dated January, 1105, in Mount Pilgrim, Raymond gave lands to the church of Arles in compensation for the ills suffered at his hands. He likewise indicated that he expected his cousin, William Jourdain, Count of Cerdagne, to carry out his wishes. The bishop of Toulon, Raymond of Baux, Décan of Posquières, Bertrand Porcelet, Raymond's wife, Elvira, and his young son, Alphonse-Jourdain, witnessed the act. Raymond lived another month, during which time he ordered Albert, former prior of Chaise-Dieu, to return the cup of Saint Robert, a relic which he had brought as a talisman on the First Crusade. Probably on February 28, 1105, Raymond of Saint-Gilles, Count of Toulouse and Count of Tripoli, died in his castle, Mount Pilgrim. Historians have pretended that William of Montpellier returned his body to the Midi, while others claim that he was buried in Jerusalem. We prefer to believe that he was buried at Mount Pilgrim, a refuge which he had established for pilgrims. He had added many titles to his first one of Count of Saint-Gilles, but toward the end he chose to style himself "comes Tholosanus vel gratia Dei Tripolitanus"; however, in reviewing his life we feel that he is best described as "Christiane milicie excellentissimus princeps." [12]

NOTES

1. Raymond d'Aguilers, *op. cit.*, p. 280; Albert of Aachen, *op. cit.*, pp. 501–503; Grousset, *op. cit.*, pp. 318–19; Jean Richard, "Note sur l'archidiocèse d'Apamée et les conquêtes de Raymond de Saint-Gilles en Syrie du Nord," in *Syria*, XXXV (1946–1948), 103–108. It seems that the sequence of events will remain a secret, and that the only recourse is to choose what appears to be the most plausible solution. This is precisely what David, Grousset, and Runciman have done. See David. *op. cit.*, p. 230.

2. Krey, *op. cit.* (*AHR*), p. 244; Hill, *op. cit.* (*Speculum*), p. 271.

3. *Kreuzzugsbriefe*, p. 173; Albert of Aachen, *op. cit.*, p. 524; *The Alexiad*, p. 287; William of Tyre, *op. cit.*, p. 417; Reinhold Röhricht, *Geschichte des Königreiches Jerusalem*, p. 34; Chalandon, *op. cit.* ("Essai"), p. 220; Fulcher, *op. cit.*, pp. 365, 368; Runciman, *op. cit.*, pp. 302–303; Runciman interprets Fulcher's remarks as an indictment of Raymond's refusal to supply food, but we cannot interpret Fulcher's remarks in this vein.

4. *Translatio S. Nicolai in Venetiam*, in *RHC Occ*, V, 271; Albert of Aachen, *op. cit.*, p. 563; Setton, *op. cit.*, p. 395.

5. Albert of Aachen, *op. cit.*, pp. 564–77.

6. Grousset, *op. cit.*, p. 327. James L. Cate, in an unpublished dis-

sertation on the Crusade of 1101 and in his chapter in *A History of the Crusades,* pp. 343–67, has an account of Raymond's actions. He is more sympathetic with Raymond's problems in this crusade and more critical of Albert's inconsistencies in his recent work.

7. Matthew of Edessa, *op. cit.,* pp. 56–57; Albert of Aachen, p. *op. cit.,* p. 583; Setton, *op. cit.,* p. 396; Runciman, *op. cit.,* II, 34. Runciman believes that Raymond limited his oath to the area north of Latakia; however, Cahen has summarized the problem. Claude Cahen, *La Syrie du Nord a l'époque des croisades,* p. 233, note 12. We know that Tancred had made plans to gain Acre earlier, and we suggest that he forced Raymond to surrender any rights which he might assert to it.

8. Albert of Aachen, *op. cit.,* p. 583; Fulcher, *op. cit.,* p. 399; Cafarus, *op. cit.,* p. 69; Röhricht, *op. cit. (Königreiches),* p. 33.

9. Jean Richard, "Le Chartrier de Sainte-Marie-Latine et l'établissement de Raymond de Saint-Gilles à Mont-Pèlerin," in *Mélanges d'histoire du Moyen Age dédiés à la mémoire de Louis Halphen,* p. 607; Ibn ah-Athīr, *op. cit.,* pp. 211–12; *The Alexiad,* p. 287; Abou'l Fedâ, *op. cit.,* p. 6.

10. Ibn al-Athīr, *op. cit.,* p. 213; *The Alexiad,* pp. 287–88; Albert of Aachen, *op. cit.,* p. 610; Richard, *op. cit. (Sainte-Marie-Latine),* pp. 608–11.

11. Cafarus, *op. cit.,* p. 70; William of Tyre, *op. cit.,* p. 441; *HGL,* V, 779–81; Reinhold Röhricht, *op. cit. (Regesta),* p. 6; Richard, *op. cit. (Sainte-Marie-Latine),* pp. 608–609.

12. Albert of Aachen, *op. cit.,* pp. 610, 623; *HGL,* III, 561–62; V, 790–93; William of Tyre, *op. cit.,* p. 452; Röhricht, *op. cit.* (Regesta), p. 8; Eugène de Rozière, *Cartulaire de l'église du Saint-Sépulchre de Jérusalem,* pp. 180–83; Ibn al-Athīr, *op. cit.,* pp. 235–36.

EPILOGUE

THROUGHOUT the First Crusade, Raymond of Saint-Gilles was the most consistent of the leaders in carrying out plans of Urban II as we understand them. Rhetorical accounts, which liken Adhémar and Raymond to Moses and Aaron, are not without a touch of reality. Like the two Biblical leaders, the bishop of Le Puy and the Count of Toulouse were to lead their people to the Promised Land, but, like their predecessors, neither was to gain the final objective. Adhémar died in Antioch, and Raymond was not made defender of the Holy Sepulcher.

In most cases, until the work of Heinrich von Sybel, historians were kind to the name of Raymond. Despite some bitter remarks interspersed in the work of his contemporaries, the majority of these authors praised him for making the First Crusade a success. Writers throughout the centuries, as late as Michaud, continued to praise the count and to emphasize his religious motives. The critical study made by von Sybel of the First Crusade brought about a school of historians who have, in most instances, portrayed the Provençal leader as a grasping old man who wished to establish his rule in many of the important towns which he besieged. Influenced by a growing materialism, they were quick to put Raymond in a modern setting. So the Count of Toulouse has been left with few friends because he has been portrayed as the cold-hearted banker of the First Crusade.

This unfortunate view cannot be explained fully by our misunderstanding of religious motivation. We know that Bohémond's ambition to rule Antioch upset Urban's hopes of co-operating with Alexius for church unity of Greeks and Latins.

After the death of Urban, Bohémond returned to Europe to launch an attack upon Alexius. The Norman leader convinced Paschal II of the justice of his cause by clever lies, which turned the minds of the Westerners against the Greeks. This doctrine put Raymond, who had cooperated with the basileus, in an unfavorable light. He became the greedy land-grabber rather than Bohémond, who saw through Greek treachery and took Antioch for the Latins. Modern scholars have often accepted this Norman propaganda.

Actually, Raymond followed consistently the pope's idea of cooperation with Alexius. It seems that the agreement of Raymond and Alexius came at a much earlier date than is generally accepted, probably during the last week of April, 1097. Later, when Bohémond advanced his claims to Antioch, Raymond reminded him of his oath to Alexius, not because he coveted the city but because he knew the value of Greek cooperation. As late as the siege of 'Arqah Raymond awaited the arrival of Alexius. Despite the charges of Raymond's greed in delaying at 'Arqah, it now seems apparent that he was the only leader in whom the people could put their trust. Whatever surmises may be made, we cannot deny that Raymond was the one chieftain who held steadfast to leading the people to Jerusalem. After what may have been a disappointment in his failure to become a defender of the Holy Sepulcher, Raymond threw his support to Godfrey against the forces of al-Afdal. When the success of the First Crusade was jeopardized by the return of weary crusaders to their homes, Raymond, still holding to his alliance with Alexius, continued to fight Moslems and to lay the foundation of the county of Tripoli, the most lasting of the Latin states in the Levant. So we may conclude with Fliche that Raymond was the only leader of the First Crusade who remained true to the spirit of the crusade.

The last decade has dealt more leniently with Raymond. His Greek policy has been evaluated and his commitments to the emperor have been defined; however, he yet suffers from the fact that his self-styled eulogist spoke a language that we have failed to grasp. Brushed by greatness, Raymond failed to capture the imagination of romanticists who later glamorized Bohémond

and Godfrey. Among contemporary or near-contemporary authors Albert lauded the pure and non-controversial Godfrey. The
author of the *Gesta* praised the able and ambitious Bohémond.
Ralph of Caen supported the Norman party and Tancred. In
so doing, their treatment of character and motive were openly
biased in their efforts to justify their heroes' actions and enlarge
their roles in the crusade.

Approaching the story from an angle other than that of the
praise of men and deeds, Raymond d'Aguilers praised the Count
of Toulouse, his master, on the one hand and damned him on
the other. In shifting his emphasis from the deeds of men to the
will of God, the chaplain likewise, in portraying the role of the
Count of Toulouse in the matter, shifted his emphasis from
objective portrayal of deeds to subjective explanations of reasons
for these actions. Thus we see the count through the concepts
of a petty churchman who exhibits that, though he may be well
versed in sin upon ritualistic levels, he cannot realistically super-
impose these notions upon the deeds of princes. In dealing with
the account of the chaplain, historians have given weight to his
self-styled closeness to the count without discounting his weak
judgment. In an uncritical way they have accepted his bad
reports of the count's conduct, without understanding the chaplain's occasional need of a protagonist for moral episodes in
his narrative. Such moralizing, when incorporated in history,
gives the character of the Count of Saint-Gilles that unrealistic
and contradictory quality which has been summed up in the word
enigmatic.

Yet, viewed through the eyes of the pro-Bohémond *Gesta,* and
divested of the ecclesiastical trappings of the chaplain, the Count
of Toulouse, judged by his deeds, appears as an intelligent
leader, who cooperated throughout the entire crusade to unite
the disorganized ranks of the army by means of councils, to aid
the poor in their hours of need, to work for Latin-Greek relations,
and, above all, to lead the Christians to the Holy Sepulcher. In
character the count appears to typify, in his practical, ruthless,
and honorable way, qualities which for other heroes were later to
be distilled and rarefied by more sensitive authors into virtues
which following centuries could applaud. Lacking such inter-

preters, we must make our own adjustments to the character and deeds of Raymond IV, Count of Toulouse, as portrayed by those primarily interested in other crusaders, or by the bungling and bigoted pen of a cleric who sought sporadically to tailor a stormy and successful warrior to the unrealistic cut of medieval allegory.

BIBLIOGRAPHY

SOURCES

Abou'l Fedâ, *Résumé de l'histoire des croisades* in *Recueil des historiens des croisades: historiens orientaux,* Vol. I, Paris, 1872. Hereafter cited *RHC Or.*

Abou'l Mehacen Youssouf, *Extraits du Nodjoûm Ex-Zahireh* in *RHC Or.,* Vol. III. Paris, 1884.

Acta sanctorum quotque toto orbe coluntur, vel a Catholicis scriptoribus celebrantur, Aprilis tomus primus. Paris and Rome, 1866.

Aelfric's Metrical Lives of Saints in *The Early English Text Society, OS,* LXXXII, edited by Walter W. Skeat. London, 1885.

Albertus Aquensis, *Historia Hierosolymitana* in *RHC: historiens occidentaux,* Vol. IV. Paris, 1879. Hereafter cited *RHC Occ.*

Alexander papa II, *Epistolae* in *Recueil des historiens des Gaules et de la France,* Vol. XIV. Paris, 1877. Hereafter cited *RHGF.*

The Alexiad of the Princess Anna Comnena, translated by Elizabeth A. S. Dawes. London, 1928.

Anonymi gesta Francorum et aliorum Hierosolymitanorum, edited by Heinrich Hagenmeyer. Heidelberg, 1890.

Arnaldus de Verdala, *Series Episcoporum Magalonensium* in *RHGF* Vol. XII. Paris, 1877.

Baldricus Dolensis, *Historia Jerosolimitana,* in *RHC Occ.,* Vol. IV. Paris, 1879.

Bartolus de Nangeio, *Gesta Francorum Iherusalem expugnantium* in *RHC Occ.,* Vol. III. Paris, 1866.

Beaumanoir, Philippe de, *Coutumes de Beauvaisis,* edited by A. Salmon. Paris, 1899.

Benjamin de Tudela, *The Itinerary of Benjamin Tudela,* translated by Marcus Nathan Adler. London, 1907.

Bernoldus Monachus S. Blasii, *Chronicon* in *Monumenta Germaniae historica*, Vol. V. Hannover, 1844. Hereafter cited *MGH SS.*

Brière, M., *Les 'homeliae cathedrales' de Sévère d'Antioche, Homélie LXXXVI*, in *Patrologia Orientalis*, Vol. XXIII. Paris, 1932.

Brunel, Clovis, *Les plus anciennes chartes en langue provençale.* Paris, 1926.

Cafarus, *De liberatione civitatum Orientis liber*, in *RHC Occ.*, Vol. V. Paris, 1895.

Cartulaire de l'abbaye de Saint-Chaffre du Monastier, edited by Ulysse Chevalier. Paris, 1884.

La chanson d'Antioche, edited by Paulin Paris, 1848, 2 vols.

La chanson du chevalier au cygne, Vol. II, edited by C. Hippeau. Paris, 1877.

Chronicon Malleacense, in *RHGF*, Vol. XII. Paris, 1877.

Chronicon monasterii S. Petri Aniciensis, in *RHGF*, Vol. XII. Paris, 1877.

Chronicon S. Martini Turonensis breve, in *RHGF*, Vol. XII. Paris, 1877.

Ekkehardus Uraugiensis abbas, *Hierosolymita*, edited by Heinrich Hagenmeyer, Tübingen, 1877.

Emerton, Ephraim, *The Correspondence of Pope Gregory VII.* New York, 1932.

Eusebius Hieronymus, *In Ezechielem* in *Patrologiae cursus completus: series latina*, edited by J. P. Migne, Vol. XXV. Paris, 1884. Hereafter cited as *MPL*.

Ex Gestis Comitum Barcinonensium, in *RHGF*, Vol. XI. Paris, 1876.

Fragmentum historiae Francicae, in *RHGF*, Vol. XI–XII. Paris, 1876, 1877.

Fulcherius Carnotensis, *Historia Iherosolymitana Gesta Francorum Iherusalem Peregrinantium*, in *RHC Occ.*, Vol. III. Paris, 1866.

Gaufredus Malaterra, *Historia Sicula*, in *MPL*, Vol. CXLIX. Paris, 1882.

Gaufredus de Briul, *Chronicon Lemovicense*, in *RHGF*, Vol. XII. Paris, 1877.

Gesta Romanorum, translated by Charles Swan. New York, 1905.

Gilo, *Historia gestorum viae nostri temporis Hierosolymitanae*, in *RHC Occ.*, Vol. V. Paris, 1895.

Gislebertus, *Chronicon Hanoniense*, in *MGH SS*, Vol. XXI. Hannover, 1869.

The Golden Legend of Jacobus de Voragine, translated by Granger Ryan and Helmut Ripperger, Vol. I. New York, 1941.

Gregory of Tours, *The History of the Franks*, translated by O. M. Dalton, Vol. II. Oxford, 1932.

Gregorius VII papa, *Registrum*, in *MPL*, Vol. CXLVIII. Paris, 1878.

Gregorius VII papa, *Concilia Romana*, in *MPL*, Vol. CXLVIII. Paris, 1878.

Guibertus Novigentus, *Historia quae dicitur Gesta Dei per Francos*, in *RHC Occ.*, Vol. IV. Paris, 1879.

Hagenmeyer, Heinrich, *Die Kreuzzugsbriefe aus den Jahren 1088–1100*. Innsbruck, 1901.

Histoire anonyme de la première croisade, edited and translated by Louis Bréhier. Paris, 1924.

Historia belli sacri, in *RHC Occ.*, Vol. III. Paris, 1866.

Ibn al-Athīr, *Extraits de la chronique intitulée Kamel-Altevarykh*, in *RHC Or.*, Vol. I. Paris, 1872.

Ibn al-Qalānisī, *The Damascus Chronicle of the Crusades*, edited and translated by H. A. R. Gibbs. London, 1932.

Itinerary from Bordeaux to Jerusalem—The Bordeaux Pilgrim, in *Palestine Pilgrim's Text Society*, Vol. I, translated by Aubrey Stewart. London, 1887.

Jacques de Vitry, *The History of Jerusalem*, in *Palestine Pilgrim's Text Society*, Vol. XI. London, 1897.

Kamāl-ad-Dīn, *Extraits de l'histoire d'Alep*, in *RHC Or.*, Vol. III. Paris, 1884.

Lambertus Hersfeldensis, *Annales*, in *MGH SS*, Vol. V. Hannover, 1844.

Liber instrumentorum memorialium: Cartulaire des Guillems de Montpellier, edited by A. Germain. Montpellier, 1884–86.

Lupus Protospatarius, *Chronicon*, in *MPL*, Vol. CLV. Paris, 1880.

Matthew of Edessa, *Extraits de la chronique de Matthieu d'Edesse*, in *RHC Arm.*, Vol. I. Paris, 1869.

Michael the Syrian, *Extrait de la chronique de Michel le Syrien*, in *RHC Arm.*, Vol. I. Paris, 1869.

Modjêr-ed-Dīn, *Histoire de Jérusalem et d'Hébron*, in *RHC Or.*, Vol. IV. Paris, 1898.

Ordericus Vitalis, *Historia ecclesiastica*, libri tredecim, in *MPL*, Vol. CLXXXVIII. Paris, 1890.

Petri Exceptiones Legum Romanorum, in Friedrich Carl von Savigny, *Geschichte des Römischen Rechts im Mittelalter*, Vol. II. Heidelberg, 1816.

Petrus Cluniacensis, *Epistolae*, in *MPL*, Vol. CLXXXIX. Paris, 1890.

Pharr, Clyde, *The Theodosian Code*. Princeton, 1952.

Rabanus Maurus, *Commentaria in Ezechielem*, in *MPL*, Vol. CX. Paris, 1884.

Radulphus Cadomensis, *Gesta Tancredi in expeditione Hierosolymitana,* in *RHC Occ.,* Vol. III. Paris, 1866.

Raimundus de Aguilers, *Historia Francorum qui ceperunt Iherusalem,* in *RHC Occ.,* Vol. III. Paris, 1866.

Regesta Regni Hierosolymitani, 1097–1291, edited by Reinhold Röhricht. Innsbruck, 1893.

Richardus Cluniacensis monachus, *Chronicon,* in *RHGF,* Vol. XII. Paris, 1877.

Robertus Monachus, *Historia Hierosolymitana,* in *RHC Occ.,* Vol. III. Paris, 1866.

Rodericus Toletanus archiepiscopus, *De rebus Hispaniae,* in *RHGF,* Vol. XII. Paris, 1877.

Rosell, Francisco M., *Liber Feudorum Maior.* Barcelona, 1945.

Rozière, E. de, *Cartulaire de l'église du Saint-Sépulchre de Jérusalem.* Paris, 1849.

Saint Ambrose, *De Officiis Ministrorum* in *MPL,* Vol. XVI. Paris, 1880.

———. "In Psalmum primum enarratio" in *Enarrationes in XII Psalmos Davidicos* in *MPL,* Vol. XIV. Paris, 1882.

Saint Augustine, De civitate Dei, in *MPL,* Vol. XLI. Paris, 1900.

Scott, Samuel P. (ed. and translator), *Las Siete Partidas.* New York, 1931.

Tardif, A. (ed.) *Coutumes de Toulouse.* Paris, 1884.

Tischendorf, Constantius de, *Biblia sacra Latina veteris Testamenti.* Lipsiae, 1873.

Translatio S. Nicolai in Venetiam in *RHC Occ.,* Vol. V. Paris, 1895.

Tudebodus, Petrus, *Historia de Hierosolymitano itinere* in *RHC Occ.,* Vol. III. Paris, 1866.

Urbain II aux princes de Flandres et à leurs sujets in *Archives de l'Orient latin,* Vol. I. Paris, 1881.

Urbanus II papa, *Epistolae et privilegia* in *MPL,* Vol. CLI. Paris, 1881.

Usatges de Barcelona, edited by Ramon d'Abadal i Vinyals et Ferran Valls Taberner. Barcelona, 1913.

The Visigothic Code (Forum Judicum), edited and translated by Samuel P. Scott. Boston, 1910.

Willelmus Malmesbiriensis, *De gestis regum Anglorum,* libri quinque, in *Rerum Britannicarum Medii Aevi Scriptores,* Vol. II, edited by William Stubbs. London, 1889.

Willelmus Tyrensis archiepiscopus, *Historia rerum in partibus transmarinis gestarum* in *RHC Occ.,* Vol. I. Paris, 1844.

William of Tyre, *A History of Deeds Done Beyond the Sea,* Vol. I, edited and translated by E. A. Babcock and A. C. Krey. New York, 1943.

Wormald, Francis, *English Kalendars before A.D. 1100,* in Henry Bradshaw Society, Vol. 72. London, 1934.

WORKS

Abbadie, François, *Le livre noir et les établissements de Dax, Archives historiques du département de la Gironde,* Vol. XXXVII. Paris-Bordeaux, 1902.

Albert, Auguste, *Éloge de Raymond IV, comte de Toulouse et de Saint-Gilles,* in *Recueil de l'Académie des Jeux Floraux.* Toulouse, 1840.

Alfaric, P., "La chanson de Sainte Foy et les croisades," *Revue des Études Historiques,* 1924.

Alphandéry, P., and Dupront, A., *La chrétienté et l'idée de croisade.* Paris, 1954.

Andressohn, J. C., *The Ancestry and Life of Godfrey of Bouillon.* Bloomington, 1947.

Auzias, Léonce, "Bernard 'Le Veau' et Bernard 'Plantevelue', Comtes de Toulouse," *Annales du Midi,* Vol. XLIV, 1932.

Baedeker, Karl, *Palestine et Syrie,* 4th edition. Leipzig, 1906.

Baldwin, M. W., "Some Recent Interpretations of Pope Urban's Eastern Policy," *The Catholic Historical Review,* Vol. XXV, 1940.

Barker, Ernest, *The Crusades.* London, 1939.

Beaumont, A. A., "Albert of Aachen and the County of Edessa," in *The Crusades and Other Historical Essays Presented to D. C. Munro.* New York, 1928.

Bédier, Joseph, *Les Légendes épiques, recherches sur la formation des chansons de geste,* Vols. I–IV. Paris, 1908–1913.

———. "Recherches sur les légendes du cycle de Guillaume d'Orange," *Annales du Midi,* Vol. XIX, 1907.

Bel, A., *Almoravids,* in *The Encyclopedia of Islam,* Vol. I. Leyden, 1913.

Bloch, Marc, *La société féodale,* Vol. I–II. Paris, 1939–40.

———. "Les formes de la rupture de l'hommage dans l'ancien droit féodale," *Revue historique de droit français,* 1912.

Boissonnade, Prosper, *Du nouveau sur la Chanson de Roland: la genèse historique, le cadre géographique, le milieu, les personnages, la date et l'auteur du poème.* Paris, 1923.

———. "Cluny, la papauté et la première grande croisade internationale contre les Sarrasins d'Espagne (1064–1065)," *Revue des questions historiques,* Vol. 117, 1932.

Bousquet, Jacques, "La donation de Ségur par Raymond de Saint-Gilles,

Comte de Toulouse, à l'Englise du Puy-en-Velay (1096)," *Annales du Midi*, 1962, no. 1.

Bréhier, Louis, *L'Église et l'Orient au Moyen Age, Les Croisades.* Paris, 1921.

————. "Adhémar de Monteil," in *Dictionnaire d'histoire et de géographie ecclésiastiques*, Vol. I. Paris, 1912.

————. "Adhémar de Monteil," in *Dictionnaire de biographie française*, Vol. III. Paris, 1931.

————. "Attempts at Reunion of the Greek and Latin Churches," in *Cambridge Medieval History*, Vol. IV. Cambridge, 1923.

————. "Les Origines des rapports entre la France et la Syrie, Le protectorat de Charlemagne," in *Congrès Français de la Syrie*, Vol. II. Marseille, 1919.

Brundage, J. A., "An Errant Crusader, Stephen of Blois," *Traditio*, Vol. XVI, 1960.

————. "Adhémar of Puy. The Bishop and his Critics," *Speculum*, Vol. XXXIV, 1959.

Cahen, Claude, *La Syrie du Nord a l'époque des Croisades.* Paris, 1940.

Calmette, Joseph, *Le monde féodal.* Paris, 1951.

————. "Les comtés et les comtes de Toulouse et de Rodez sous Charles le Chauve," *Annales du Midi*, Vol. XVII, 1905.

————. "La dynastie raymondine et le comté de Tripoli, a propos d'un ouvrage récent," *Annales du Midi*, Vol. LXI, 1948–49.

Cate, J. L., "A Gay Crusader," *Byzantion*, Vol. XVI, 1942–43.

Chalandon, Ferdinand, *Essai sur le règne d'Alexis Iᵉʳ Comnène (1081–1118).* Paris, 1900.

————. *Histoire de la domination normande en Italie et en Sicile*, Vol. I. Paris, 1907.

————. *Histoire de la première croisade jusqu'a l'élection de Godefroi de Bouillon.* Paris, 1925.

Charanis, Peter, "A Greek Source on the Origin of the First Crusade," *Speculum*, Vol. XXIV, 1949.

Charlesworth, Martin Percival, *Trade Routes and Commerce of the Roman Empire.* Cambridge, 1926.

Craig, James A., *The Jus Feudale.* London, 1930.

Crégut, G. Regis, *Le concile de Clermont en 1095 et la première croisade.* Clermont-Ferrand, 1895.

Crozet, René, "Le Voyage d'Urbain II en France (1095–1096) et son importance au point de vue archéologique," *Annales du Midi*, Vol. XLIX, 1937.

————. "Le voyage d'Urbain II et ses négociations avec le clergé de France (1095–1096)," *Revue Historique*, Vol. CLXXIX, 1937.

Daly, William, "Christian Fraternity, the Crusaders, and the Security of Constantinople, 1097–1204: The Precarious Survival of an Ideal," *Medieval Studies,* Vol. XXII, 1960.

David, Charles W., *Robert Curthose, Duke of Normandy.* Cambridge, 1920.

Defourneaux, M., *Les Français en Espagne aux XIe et XIIe siècles.* Paris, 1949.

Delbrück, Hans, *Geschichte der Kriegskunst im Rahmen der politischen Geschichte,* Dritter Teil, *Das Mittelalter,* Berlin, 1907.

Delpech, Henri, *La tactique au XIIIe siècle,* Vol. II. Paris, 1886.

Deschamps, Paul, *Les châteaux des croisés en Terre Sainte: le Crac des Chevaliers.* Paris, 1934.

Devic, Dom. Cl. and Vaissete, Dom. J., *Histoire générale de Languedoc,* edited by Privat, 15 vols. Toulouse, 1872–93.

Diehl, Charles, *History of the Byzantine Empire,* translated by George B. Ives. Princeton, 1925.

Dozy, Reinhart P. A., *Recherches sur l'histoire et la littérature de l'Espagne pendant le Moyen Age,* Vol. II. Leyden, 1881.

———. *Spanish Islam, A History of the Moslems in Spain,* translated by Francis G. Stokes. New York, 1913.

Duncalf, Frederic, "The Pope's Plan for the First Crusade," in *The Crusades and Other Historical Essays Presented to Dana C. Munro.* New York, 1928.

Duprat, Eugène, "Les Relations de la Provence et du Levant, du Ve siècle aux Croisades," in *Congrès Français de la Syrie,* Vol. II, 1919.

Dussaud, René, *Topographie historique de la Syrie antique et médiévale.* Paris, 1927.

Erdmann, C., *Die Entstehung des Kreuzzugsgedankens.* Stuttgart, 1935.

Esmein, A., *Le mariage en droit canonique.* Paris, 1891.

Fauriel, Claude-Charles, *Histoire de la poésie provençale.* Paris, 1846.

Flach, Jacques, *Les origines de l'ancienne France, X^e et XIe siècles,* Vol. IV. Paris, 1917.

Fleury, Ch. Rohault de, *Mémoire sur les instruments de la Passion de Notre-Seigneur Jésus-Christ.* Paris, 1870.

Fliche, Augustin, "L'élection d'Urbain II," *Le Moyen Age,* Vol. XIX, 1915.

———. "Urbain II et la croisade," *Revue d'Histoire de l'Église de France,* Vol. XIV, 1927.

———. "L'Europe occidentale de 888 à 1125," *Histoire du Moyen Age,* Vol. II, edited by Gustave Glotz. Paris, 1930.

Gallia Christiana in provincias ecclesiasticus distributa, Vols. I–V. Paris, 1870–77.

Gierke, Otto, *Political Theories of the Middle Ages,* translated by F. W. Maitland. Cambridge, 1938.

Gieyztor, Alexander, "The Genesis of the Crusades. The Encyclical of Sergius IV, 1009–1012," *Medievalia et Humanistica,* Vol. VI, 1950.

Glaesener, Henri, "L'Escalade de la tour d'Antioche," *Revue du Moyen Age Latin,* Vol. II, 1946.

———. "Godefroy de Bouillon et la bataille de l'Ester," *Revue des Etudes Historiques,* 1938.

Grousset, René, *Histoire des croisades et du royaume franc de Jérusalem,* 3 vols. Paris, 1934–36.

Hagenmeyer, Heinrich, "Chronologie de la première croisade, 1094–1100," *Revue de l'Orient Latin,* Vols. VI–VIII, 1902–1911.

Heerman, Otto, *Die Gefechtsführung der abendländischen Heere im Orient in der Epoche des ersten Kreuzzuges.* Marburg, 1887.

Heyd, Wilhelm, *Histoire du commerce du Levant au Moyen Age,* Vol. II. Leipzig, 1886.

Hill, John Hugh, "Raymond of Saint-Gilles in Urban's Plan of Greek and Latin Friendship," *Speculum,* Vol. XXVI, 1951.

Hill, John Hugh and Laurita L., "Contemporary Accounts and the Later Reputation of Adhémar, Bishop of Le Puy," *Medievalia et Humanistica,* Vol. IX, 1955.

———. "Justification historique du titre de Raymond de Saint-Gilles: 'Christiane milicie excellentissimus princeps,'" *Annales du Midi,* Vol. LXVI, 1954.

———. "L'allégorie chrétienne dans les récits relatifs au Wineland," *Le Moyen Age,* N. 1–2, 1960.

———. "The Convention of Alexius Comnenus and Raymond of Saint-Gilles," *American Historical Review,* Vol. LVIII, 1953.

A History of the Crusades, directed by Kenneth M. Setton and Marshall W. Baldwin. Philadelphia, 1955.

Hitti, Philip K., *History of the Arabs.* London, 1937.

Holmes, Urban Tigner, *A History of Old French Literature from the Origins to 1300.* New York, 1937.

Howorth, Sir Henry H., *Saint Gregory the Great.* London, 1912.

Jaffé, Philippus, *Regesta pontificum Romanorum ab condita ecclesia ad annum post Christum natum,* MCXCVIII primus. Lipsiae, 1885.

Jaurgain, Jean de, *La Vasconie, étude historique et critique sur les origines du royaume de Navarre, du duché de Gascogne, des comtés de Comminges d'Aragon, de Foix, de Bigorre, d'Alava et de Biscaye, de la vicomté de Béarn et des grand fiefs du duché de Gascogne,* Vol. II. Pau, 1902.

Jeanroy, A., "Les troubadours en Espagne," *Annales du Midi*, Vols. XXVII–XXVIII, 1915–16.

Johnson, R. L., Review, *Byzantinoslavica*, Vol. XII, 1951.

Jones, E. C., *Saint-Gilles: essai d'histoire littéraire*. Paris, 1914.

Joranson, Einor, "The Alleged Frankish Protectorate in Palestine," *American Historical Review*, Vol. XXXII, 1927.

Klein, Clemens, *Raimund von Aguilers, Quellenstudie zur Geschichte des ersten Kreuzzuges*. Berlin, 1892.

Knappen, Marshall M., "Robert II of Flanders in the First Crusade," in *The Crusades and Other Historical Essays Presented to Dana C. Munro*. New York, 1928.

Kohler, Ch. *Mélanges pour servir à l'histoire de l'Orient latin et des croisades*. Paris, 1906.

Krey, August C., "A Neglected Passage in the *Gesta* and its Bearing on the Literature of the First Crusade," in *The Crusades and Other Historical Essays Presented to Dana C. Munro*. New York, 1928.

———. "Urban's Crusade, Success or Failure?" in *American Historical Review*, Vol. LIII, 1948.

Krueger, Hilmar C., "Genoese Trade with Northwest Africa in the Twelfth Century," *Speculum*, Vol. VIII, 1933.

Kügler, Bernhard, *Albert von Aachen*. Stuttgart, 1885.

———. *Bohemund und Tankred*. Tübingen, 1862.

La Monte, John L., "Byzantine Empire and Crusading States," *Byzantion*, Vol. VII, 1932.

Langlade, Jacques, *L'abbaye de la Chaise-Dieu*. Paris, 1923.

Lea, Henry Charles, *Superstition and Force*. Philadelphia, 1892.

Leib, Bernard, *Rome, Kiev et Byzance à la fin du XIe siècle, rapports religieux des Latins et des Gréco-Russes sous le pontificat d'Urbain II (1080–1099)*. Paris, 1924.

Lemaire, André, "La *dotatio* de l'épouse, de l'époque mérovingienne au XIIIe siècle," *Revue historique de droit français*, 4e serie, Vol. XIV, 1935.

Longnon, Jean, *Les Français d'outre-mer au Moyen Age, essai sur l'expansion française dans le bassin de la Méditerranée*. Paris, 1920.

Luchaire, Achille, *Histoire des institutions monarchiques de la France sous les premiers Capétiens (987–1180)*, Vol. II. Paris, 1891.

MacKinney, Loren C., "The People and Public Opinion in the Eleventh Century Peace Movement," *Speculum*, Vol. V, 1930.

Manteyer, Georges de, *La Provence du Ier au XIIe siècle*. Paris, 1908.

Marianna, John de, *The General History of Spain*, translated by Captain John Stevens. London, 1699.

Maury, Alfred, *Croyances et légendes du Moyen Âge*. Paris, 1896.

Mayer, Hans Eberhard, "Zur Beurteilung Adhémars von Le Puy," *Deutsches Archiv*, no. 2, 1960.

———. Review, *Deutsches Archiv*, no. 2, 1960.

———. Review, *Gottingische Gelehrte Anzeigen*, N. 1–2, 1960.

———. "Zum Tode Wilhelms von Tyrus," *Archiv für Diplomatick*, 1959–60.

Michaud, Joseph F., *Histoire des croisades*, Vol. I. Paris, 1896.

Munro, Dana C., "The Speech of Pope Urban II at Clermont, 1095," *American Historical Review*, Vol. XI, 1906.

———. "The Western Attitude toward Islam during the Crusades," *Speculum*, Vol. VII, 1932.

Nicholson, Robert Lawrence, *Tancred: A Study of His Career and Work in Their Relation to the First Crusade and the Establishment of the Latin States in Syria and Palestine*. Chicago, 1940.

Norden, Walter, *Das Papsttum und Byzanz: die Trennung der beiden Mächte und das Problem ihrer Wiedervereinigung bis zum Untergange des byzantinischen Reichs (1453)*. Berlin, 1903.

Papon, Jean-Pierre, *Histoire générale de Provence*, Vol. II. Paris, 1778.

Paris, Gaston, "Le chanson du pèlerinage de Charlemagne," *Romania*, Vol. IX, 1880.

Paulot, Lucien, *Un pape français: Urbain II*. Paris, 1903.

Petit, Ernest, "Croisades bourguignonnes contre les Sarrazins d'Espagne au XIᵉ siècle," *Revue Historique*, Vol. XXX, 1886.

Pirenne, Henri, *Mohammed and Charlemagne*, New York, 1939.

Porges, Walter, "The Clergy, the Poor, and the Non-Combatants on the First Crusade," *Speculum*, Vol. XXI, 1946.

Poupardin, René, *Le royaume de Provence sous les Carolingiens (855–933)*. Paris, 1901.

Prou, Maurice, *La Gaule Mérovingienne*. Paris, 1897.

Rey, Edouard G., *Les familles d'outre-mer, de du Cange*. Paris, 1869.

Rey, Emmanuel G., *Les colonies franques de Syrie aux XIIᵉ et XIIIᵉ siècles*. Paris, 1883.

Riant, Paul, Comte, "Inventaire critique des lettres historiques des croisades," *Archives de l'Orient latin*, Vol. I, 1881.

Richard, Alfred, *Histoire des comtes de Poitou*, 2 vols. Paris, 1903.

Richard, Jean, *Le comté de Tripoli sous la dynastie toulousaine (1102–1187)*. Paris, 1945.

———. *Le royaume latin de Jérusalem*. Paris, 1953.

———. "Colonies marchandes privilégiées et marché seigneurial. La fonde d'Acre et ses 'droitures,'" *Le Moyen Age*, 1953.

———. "Le Chartrier de Sainte-Marie-Latine et l'établissement de Raymond de Saint-Gilles à Mont-Pèlerin," *Mélanges d'histoire du Moyen Age dédiés à la mémoire de Louis Halphen*. Paris, 1951.

———. "Note sur l'archidiocèse d'Apamée et les conquêtes de Raymond de Saint-Gilles en Syrie du Nord," *Syria*, Vol. XXV, 1946–48.

Richardot, Hubert, "Le fief roturier à Toulouse aux XIIᵉ et XIIIᵉ siècles," *Revue historique de droit francais*, 4ᵉ serie, Vol. XIV, 1935.

Röhricht, Reinhold, *Geschichte des ersten Kreuzzuges*. Innsbruck, 1901.

———. *Geschichte des Königreiches Jerusalem (1100–1291)*. Innsbruck, 1898.

Rousset, P., *Les origines et les caractères de la première croisade*. Neuchâtel, 1945.

Rowe, John Gordon, "The Papacy and the Ecclesiastical Province of Tyre (1100–1187)," *Bulletin of the John Rylands Library*, Vol. XLIII, 1960.

———. "The Papacy and the Greeks (1122–1153)," *Church History*, Vol. XXVIII, 1959.

Ruinart, Thierri, *Vita Urbani* in *MPL*, Vol. CLI. Paris, 1881.

Runciman, Steven, *A History of the Crusades*, Vols. I–II. Cambridge, 1951–52.

———. "The Byzantine 'Protectorate' in the Holy Land in the XI Century," *Byzantion*, Vol. XIX, 1948.

———. "First Crusaders' Journey Across the Balkans," *Byzantion*, 1949.

———. "The Holy Lance Found at Antioch," *Analecta Bollandiana*, Vol. LXVIII, 1950.

———. Review, *English Historical Review*, Vol. LXXVI, 1961.

Sackur, Ernest, *Die Cluniacenser*, 2 vols. Halle, 1892.

Saint-Yon, Moline de, *Histoire des comtes de Toulouse*, Vol. II. Paris, 1859–61.

Schäfer, Dietrich, "Honor, citra, cis im Mittelalterlichen Latein," *Sitzungsberichte der Preussischen Akademie der Wissenschaften*, Berlin, 1921.

Schaube, Adolf, *Handelsgeschichte der romanischen Völker des Mittelmeergebieets bis zum Ende der Kreuzzüge*. Berlin, 1906.

"Séances de travaux: l'abbaye de Saint-Victor et la Palestine aux temps des croisades," *Congrès français de la Syrie*, 1919.

Smail, R. C., *Crusading Warfare (1097–1193). A Contribution to Medieval Military History*. Cambridge, 1956.

Smith, Charles E., *Papal Enforcement of Some Medieval Marriage Laws*. Baton Rouge, 1940.

Smith, L. M., *Cluny in the Eleventh and Twelfth Centuries*. London, 1930.

Stevenson, William B., *The Crusaders in the East*. Cambridge, 1907.

Sybel, Heinrich von, *Geschichte des ersten Kreuzzuges*. Leipzig, 1881.

——. *The History and Literature of the Crusades*, translated by Lady Duff Gordon. London, 1861.

Thibaut, L., Review, *Provence Historique*, Vol. X, 1960.

Thompson, James Westfall, *Economic and Social History of the Middle Ages (300–1300)*. New York, 1928.

Thorpe, Benjamin, editor and translator, *The Homilies of the Anglo-Saxon Church*, 2 vols. London, 1844–46.

Tournier, Mgr. Clément, "La première croisade, Raymond IV, comte de Toulouse, et Saint Sernin," *Revue historique de Toulouse*, 1946.

Vachez, Antoine, *Les familles chevaleresques du Lyonnais, Forez, et Beaujolais, croisades*. Lyon, 1875.

Vasiliev, Alexander A., *History of the Byzantine Empire*, 2e edition. Oxford, 1952.

Villey, M. *La Croisade. Essai sur la formation d'une théorie juridique*. Paris, 1942.

Vinogradoff, Sir P., *The Growth of the Manor*. London, 1920.

Wass, A., *Geschichte der Kreuzzüge*. Freiburg, 1956.

Wolff, Robert Lee, "Romania: The Latin Empire of Constantinople," *Speculum*, Vol. XIII, 1948.

Wright, John Kirtland, *The Geographical Lore of the Time of the Crusades*. New York, 1925.

Yewdale, Ralph Bailey, *Bohemond I, Prince of Antioch*. Princeton, 1917.

INDEX

COLOPHON

This book has been set in 10 point Linotype Baskerville, leaded 2 points, using 12 point Baskerville caps and 36 point Deepdene Italic for display. The book is printed on 60 pound P.H. Glatfelter antique standard white text, R grade, and bound in Holliston embossed "DF" Roxite, over 80 point binders board. Manufactured by the Vail-Ballou Press, Inc.